George Du Maurier

Twayne's English Authors Series

Herbert Sussman, Editor

Northeastern University

TEAS 355

GEORGE DU MAURIER
(1834 – 1896)

George Du Maurier

By Richard Kelly

University of Tennessee

Twayne Publishers • Boston

George Du Maurier

Richard Kelly

Copyright © 1983 by G. K. Hall & Company
All Rights Reserved
Published by Twayne Publishers
A Division of G. K. Hall & Company
70 Lincoln Street
Boston, Massachusetts 02111

Book Production by John Amburg
Book Design by Barbara Anderson

Printed on permanent/durable acid-free
paper and bound in the United States of
America.

Library of Congress Cataloging in Publication Data

Kelly, Richard.
  George Du Maurier.

  (Twayne's English authors series : TEAS 355)
  Bibliography: p. 168
  Includes Index.
    1. Du Maurier, George Louis Palmella Busson, 1834–1896.
2. Authors, English—19th century—Biography.   3. Illus-
trators—Great Britain—Biography.   I. Title.   II. Series.
PR4636.K44   1983   823'.8 [B]   82-15683
ISBN 0-8057-6841-6

Contents

About the Author

Richard Kelly holds a B.A. from the City College of New York and an M.A. and Ph.D. from Duke University. His specialty is Victorian humor and poetry. He has written *Douglas Jerrold*, *Lewis Carroll*, and *The Andy Griffith Show*, and edited *The Best of Mr. Punch: the Humorous Writings of Douglas Jerrold*. He has also published articles on Lewis Carroll, Robert Browning, Lord Chesterfield, and Samuel Johnson.

Since 1965 he has been a member of the English faculty at the University of Tennessee, Knoxville, where he is now professor of English and director of Graduate Studies in English. He is currently working on a collection of the drawings of George Du Maurier and on a critical study of the writings of Graham Greene.

Preface

Almost everyone has heard of Svengali, but hardly anyone today remembers his creator, George Du Maurier. Nevertheless, *Trilby*, the novel in which Svengali appears, was one of the best-selling books in the nineteenth century. Moreover, its author was one of the foremost illustrators of his day before he turned late in life to writing novels. He delighted readers of *Punch* for over thirty years with his keen satirical drawings of upper-class English society. His literary and artistic friendships included Henry James, Kate Greenaway, John Everett Millais, James McNeill Whistler, George Eliot, G. H. Lewes, Sir Walter Besant, William Allingham, and Edward Poynter. His work was widely known in America as well as in England because he published his three novels first in the United States. Furthermore, Henry James strongly promoted both Du Maurier's drawings and fiction in three major essays in American magazines. Despite the distinguished reputation he enjoyed in his lifetime, however, Du Maurier has received scant attention in the twentieth century. His name has been kept alive mainly by his granddaughter, Daphne Du Maurier, the well-known gothic mystery writer.

There has not been an extended study of Du Maurier's work since the publication of Leonée Ormond's definitive biography in 1969, and there has never appeared a thorough critical examination of his novels. The present volume, it is hoped, will fill this gap and stimulate further study of Du Maurier's neglected fiction. The principal aim of this book, then, is to present a comprehensive critical and analytical discussion of Du Maurier's three novels, *Peter Ibbetson*, *Trilby*, and *The Martian*. In order to place these novels in their proper context, I have in the first chapter examined Du Maurier's life and times and in the second chapter discussed his work as an artist. As will be shown, Du Maurier's thirty years as an artist-illustrator provided him a unique apprenticeship toward becoming a novelist, and no study of his fiction, therefore, would be complete unless it took into account the important relationships between his drawings and his novels.

For helping me in my study, I would like to thank the Trustees of the John C. Hodges Fund for granting me a mini-sabbatical to complete the writing of this book.

Richard Kelly

University of Tennessee

Chronology

1834 George Louis Palmella Busson Du Maurier born on March 6, in Paris; son of Louis-Mathurin Du Maurier and Ellen Clarke Du Maurier.

1842 Du Maurier family moves to Passy, where George attends the Pension Froussard.

1851 Fails his baccalaureat examination. Family moves to Pentonville, outside of London. George enrolls as student at the Birbeck Chemical Laboratory of University College to study chemistry.

1853 First meets Emma Wightwick.

1856 June 8, death of his father. George returns to Paris and enrolls in the atelier of Charles Gleyre. Meets Thomas Lamont, Thomas Armstrong, Edward Poynter, and James Whistler.

1857 Moves to Antwerp where he enrolls in the Academy of Fine Arts. Meets Felix Moscheles and experiments with mesmerism. Loses sight in his left eye; moves with his mother to Malines for medical treatment. Meets Carry, the model for Trilby.

1859 Receives definitive diagnosis that he will never regain vision in his left eye.

1860 Moves to London in search of a career as illustrator; drawings accepted in *Once A Week*; in October *Punch* publishes his first cartoon.

1861 Publishes "Recollections of an English Gold Mine" in *Once A Week*. Introduced to high society by Alexander Ionides. Proposes marriage to Emma Wightwick.

1862 Enters the intellectual and cultural circle of the Val Prinsep family.

1863 January 3, marries Emma Wightwick.

1864 Joins the staff of *Punch*. Daughter, Beatrix, born.

1865   Son, Guy Louis, born.

1866   First major work, "A Legend of Camelot," appears in *Punch*. Illustrates the *Ingoldsby Legends*. Daughter, Sylvia Jocelyn, born.

1867   Illustrates *The Story of a Feather*.

1868   Illustrates *Henry Esmond*. Daughter, Marie Louise, born.

1869   Moves with his wife and children from London to Hampstead. Meets George Eliot, G. H. Lewes, and Kate Greenaway.

1873   Birth of Gerald, his fifth and last child. Begins satiric drawings of aesthetes for *Punch* that run until 1882.

1874   Relocates family to New Grove House, Hampstead, where they reside for the next twenty years. Begins a series of eleven cartoons on blue-and-white china craze for *Punch*, the last drawing appearing in 1877.

1875   Acquires St. Bernard named Chang, drawings of which soon appear in *Punch*.

1878   Publishes prose narrative, "Rise and Fall of Jack Spratts," in *Punch*.

1880   Illustrates *Washington Square* and develops friendship with Henry James. His drawings for *Punch* published in a volume entitled *English Society at Home: From the Collection of Mr. Punch*.

1889   Begins writing *Peter Ibbetson* in March and completes it during the summer.

1890   Publishes "The Illustration of Books from the Serious Artist's Point of View" in the *Magazine of Art*.

1891   *Peter Ibbetson* published in *Harper's Monthly Magazine* from June to December; a two-volume book edition published without illustrations by Harper's; a one-volume edition with illustrations by Du Maurier published by Osgood McIlvaine.

1892   A two-volume edition of *Peter Ibbetson* with illustrations published by Osgood McIlvaine. Begins work on *Trilby*.

1894   *Trilby* published in *Harper's Monthly Magazine* between January and July. Whistler brings libel suit against Harper's; Du Maurier begins writing *The Martian*. *Trilby* published in book form by Harper's.

1895   *Trilby* adapted for the stage by Paul Potter; first produced in March by A. M. Palmer at the Boston Museum, and in October by Beerbohm Tree at the Haymarket Theatre in London. Du Mauriers move to Oxford Square, near Hyde Park.

1896   Dies of congestive heart failure on October 8. *The Martian* published in *Harper's Monthly Magazine* from October 1896 to July 1897.

1897   *The Martian* published in book form by Harper's.

1898   *Social Pictorial Satire* published in *Harper's Monthly Magazine* from February to March.

DELICATE CONSIDERATION.

Mamma. "WHAT A DIN YOU'RE MAKING, CHICKS! WHAT *ARE* YOU PLAYING AT?"

Trixy. "O, MAMMA, WE'RE PLAYING AT RAILWAY TRAINS. I'M THE ENGINE, AND GUY'S A FIRST-CLASS CARRIAGE, AND SYLVIA'S A SECOND-CLASS CARRIAGE, AND MAY'S A THIRD-CLASS CARRIAGE, AND GERALD, HE'S A THIRD-CLASS CARRIAGE, TOO— THAT IS, HE'S REALLY ONLY A *TRUCK*, YOU KNOW, ONLY YOU MUSTN'T TELL HIM SO, AS IT WOULD OFFEND HIM!"

DELICATE CONSIDERATION

Emma Du Maurier and her five children. *Punch*, 1873.

Chapter One
Life and Time
Passy

Robert Mathurin Busson, the grandfather of George Du Maurier, was a master glassblower who fled to England from his native France in 1789 to avoid a charge of fraud. Financially incompetent but socially ambitious, he created a fictional, aristocratic past for himself and added "Du Maurier" to his name to bolster his elevated new image. He worked for a time as a craftsman for the Whitefriar's glass company in London, but his wild speculative schemes soon led him to prison where, one imagines, he entertained his fellow inmates with stories of his former nobility. By 1802 he had sired six children, but the responsibility of supporting such a large family overwhelmed him, and he fled to France where he remained as a schoolmaster until his death in 1811.

Robert Busson's fourth child, Louis-Mathurin Busson Du Maurier, the father of George Du Maurier, was born in 1797. When he was eighteen his mother moved the family from London to Paris where Louis-Mathurin enrolled in a school to study opera. Although he possessed a beautiful voice, he abandoned an operatic career for the more quixotic life of an inventor. As such he was not unlike Lewis Carroll's White Knight, for in his son's words, "He was a man of scientific tastes, and lost his money in inventions which never came to anything."[1]

In 1831 Louis-Mathurin married Ellen Clarke, the daughter of Mary-Anne Clarke, a notorious courtesan of the Regency. Like his father, Louis kept his family on the perpetual brink of poverty. He squandered what little money he earned, his inventions were practical failures, and yet he and Ellen nourished a childlike fantasy that one day they would suddenly become prosperous. According to Leonée Ormond, their eldest son George was born "while their illusions were

I

still fresh, and they communicated to him the dream world which they inhabited."[2] They also left him a lifelong believer in his family's aristocratic roots. George grew up believing that his family line went back to twelfth-century France and that his grandfather had owned estates there but had been driven into exile in England during the French Revolution.

George Louis Palmella Busson Du Maurier was born in Paris on March 6, 1834. Besides the fabrication of nobility in the "Du Maurier," the "Palmella" was included as a compliment to a wealthy Portuguese nobleman, the duke of Palmella, whose wife was a friend of Louis-Mathurin's sister. As Ormond notes, George's birth proved to be a tale of two countries: "From the first, George Du Maurier was subject to a conflict between his two nationalities. He was not only half-French and half-English, but the grandchild of a Frenchman exiled in England, and of an Englishwoman exiled in France." Thus, she concludes, "The aching nostalgia, which characterized his personality, had its roots as much in the family history as in his own memories of childhood."[3] The two cultures that he embodied were reinforced when, as a very young child, he learned to read and speak French and English with equal ease. The effect of this cultural melange was to create a powerful duality in Du Maurier's character that was finally to assert itself in his novels, where the theme of the split personality is dominant.

Soon after the birth of George, the Du Mauriers moved to Brussels where in 1836, Louis-Mathurin, with the help of the duke of Palmella, became a scientific advisor to the Portuguese embassy. Unstable as ever, he lost this post within a year and moved his family to London. They now had a second son, Eugene, and in 1839 their first daughter, Isabella Louise, was born. It was not long, however, before Ellen's mother, Mary-Anne Clarke, invited her daughter and children to stay with her in Boulogne, an arrangement that lasted for three years. Louis-Mathurin, meantime, returned to his scientific studies in Paris. He again ventured into several business speculations that failed and, gypsylike, moved his family in 1842 to Passy, a tranquil suburb of Paris. Still restless, the family moved in and out of several homes and apartments in the area between 1842 and 1846, the Rue de la Pompe providing the fondest memories for the young dreamer, George.

The early chapters of George Du Maurier's first novel, *Peter Ibbetson*, recall with a vivid pastoral charm these years at Passy. In the opening pages he describes a large private park, a short distance from his home, that he remembers as an unspoiled paradise:

All this vast enclosure (full of strange singing, humming, whistling, buzzing, twittering, cooing, booming, croaking, flying, creeping, crawling, jumping, climbing, burrowing, splashing, diving things) had been neglected for ages—an Eden where one might gather and eat the fruit of the tree of knowledge without fear, and learn lovingly the ways of life without losing one's innocence; a forest that had remade for itself a new virginity, and become primeval once more; when beautiful Nature had reasserted her own sweet will, and massed and tangled everything together as though a Beauty had been sleeping there undisturbed for close on a hundred years, and was only waiting for the Charming Prince.[4]

At Passy, George felt at one with the world, with his family, and with himself, and his memories of that delightful town left "Kicky" (as he was called) with an indelible imprint of lost youth and joy. As his famous granddaughter, Daphne Du Maurier, notes, "All the familiar sounds and scents of Louis-Philippe's Paris, his pleasant bourgeois Paris, that filled Kicky's small ears and nostrils in those early years were to be stored up and remembered with a strange yearning, an almost unbearable sense of nostalgia, half a century later."[5]

George attended a day school across the street from his home, but his mother felt that his education there was inadequate and sent him and his brother to an expensive boarding school called the Pension Froussard. Daphne describes her grandfather at this period in his life: "He longed to be very tall, and immensely strong, and the handsomest boy in the school, and it was his misfortune that he was slightly smaller than medium height, not particularly muscular, and, now that his fair curls had become brown and straight and his apple cheeks sallow, he was not even very good looking."[6] The balance between fantasy and reality was difficult for him to maintain as a fourteen-year-old boy, and he eagerly gave himself over to romantic daydreams of superhuman accomplishments. The good days at the Pension Froussard, the pranks and escapades of youth, are vividly recorded in George's third novel, *The Martian*, many years later. He found his studies, however, both difficult and unpleasant, and complains bitterly in the novel about having to study the classics. What he prized above all in his reading were the romantic adventures found in the works of Alexander Dumas, Victor Hugo, Sir Walter Scott, François Villon, and Pierre de Ronsard. As an adult he continued to turn to the exotic beauty of the past for inspiration for both his illustrations and novels.

Real-life adventure, however, came perilously near his doorstep in 1848, with the revolution that deposed Louis Philippe. Late in February fighting broke out in Paris and the Pension Froussard was close enough to allow the boys to hear the gunfire and to see the houses burning on the horizon. All of the students were instructed to sleep on the floors to be out of the line of fire in the event that stray bullets passed through the windows. No harm ever came to anyone at the school, but one can easily imagine the wide eyes and cocked ears of all the young boys as they shared this exciting adventure together through the night.

In 1851 George faced the grim reality of the baccalaureat, the examination prerequisite to graduation. His fondness for romantic novels over the classics, and his habit of daydreaming, alas, did not go far in preparing him for the examination, and he failed to pass it. The Latin paper proved too difficult for him. His mother was greatly displeased with him but his father accepted the failure with good humor and saw to it that he continue his education elsewhere. He helped his son get enrolled at the Birbeck Chemical Laboratory of University College, London, to study chemistry.

Pentonville

The entire family moved to England and settled in an apartment in Pentonville. George became miserable with his new life, as Daphne Du Maurier points out: "Kicky was going through rather a difficult period. He hated his surroundings for one thing—the grey-drab respectability of Pentonville, and the dreary apartment where they lived."[7] Furthermore, he took no pleasure in his studies at the Birbeck Laboratory, where his work was monotonous and his fellow students were boisterous and crude-minded. His mother describes him at this time: "He has no initiative, no energy. He sits about and dreams. Always a pencil in his hand—and I think of the money wasted on his education."[8]

He simply did not have the temperament of a scientist. Lacking in patience and curiosity, he turned from his boring chemicals to draw amusing caricatures of fellow students and teachers. His new dream at this time, however, was not to become an artist but an opera singer. His father's fine singing voice and love of opera were the obvious inspiration, but George's voice proved to be inadequate for serious training. His love for music, nevertheless, remained with him throughout his life and is clearly reflected in his drawings and novels.

The intense displeasure George felt toward Pentonville was soon focused in upon himself, and he describes his loss of self confidence in *Peter Ibbetson*: "I loathed the very sight of myself in the shop windows as I went by; and yet I always looked for it there, in the forlorn hope of at least finding some alteration, even for the worse. I passionately longed to be somebody else; and yet I never met anybody else I could have borne to be for a moment."[9] He thus retreated to a world of fantasy, music, and art in order to escape his surroundings and his own hateful self-image. He frequented the British Museum, the National Gallery, and Covent Garden. Peter Ibbetson, sitting in the gallery of the theater, remarks, "Then lo! the curtain rises, and straightway we are in Seville—Seville, after Pentonville!"[10] George would also walk down to the London Bridge to watch the steamer leave for Boulogne. Filled with self-pity and unhappiness, eighteen-year-old George saw little joy or purpose in the world and began to develop a cynical attitude toward religion. He boldly declared himself an agnostic and for the rest of his life he enjoyed making occasional attacks upon orthodox Christianity.

George finally found new interests to lift him from his despondency. In 1852 he began to expand his aristic talent by drawing the various sculptures in the British Museum. In the following year his sister Isabella introduced him to Emma Wightwick, who would become his wife a decade later. George, however, was not much interested in women at this time and began a series of holiday excursions to Milford and Norfolk. His restlessness was temporarily halted when, in 1856, his father died. Louis-Mathurin's love of music apparently did not desert him even at the hour of his death, for it is reported that he died in his son's arms while singing one of Count de Segur's drinking songs.[11] The story may be apocryphal, but such a melodramatic deathbed scene was in keeping with Louis-Mathurin's character. Shortly after his funeral, his family abandoned Pentonville to return to Paris, where George had determined to study at one of the famous art schools.

Paris

Leaving London by steamer, George was delighted to see the years in Pentonville fall behind him. He describes the cheerful moment in *Peter Ibbetson*: "I stood by the man at the wheel, and saw St. Paul's and London Bridge and the Tower fade out of sight; with what hope and joy I cannot describe. I almost forgot that I was me."[12] Now twenty-two years old, George looked toward Paris as the city of his dreams, a place where his artistic talents could at last be nurtured and where he could begin to test and understand his own identity.

Once in Paris he soon enrolled in the atelier of Charles Gleyre, a Swiss painter in the tradition of Jean Ingres. Gleyre preached the importance of line over color, and insisted upon skillful drawing as the basis for art. George's experiences at his studies and the atelier are warmly and affectionately described in *Trilby*. The studio itself is bright, homely, and crowded with memorable art objects:

Along the walls, at a great height, ran a broad shelf, on which were other casts in plaster, terracotta, imitation bronze: a little Theseus, a little Venus of Milo, a little discobolus; a little flayed man threatening high heaven (an act that seemed almost pardonable under the circumstances!); a lion and a boar by Barye; an anatomical figure of a horse with only one leg left and no ears; a horse's head from the pediment of the Parthenon, earless also; and the bust of Clytie, with her beautiful low brow, her sweet wan gaze, and the ineffable forward shrug of her dear shoulders that makes her bosom a nest, a rest, a pillow, a refuge—to be loved and desired forever by generation after generation of the sons of men.[13]

The room exhibits a charm and vitality that reflect the character of its tenants. Besides the works of art "there were alcoves, recesses, irregularities, odd little nooks and corners, to be filled up as time wore on with endless personal knick-knacks, bibelots, private properties and acquisitions—things that make a place genial, homelike, and good to remember, and sweet to muse upon (with fond regret) in afteryears."[14]

Gleyre's atelier was filled with a fascinating variety of young men, a fraternity joined together by their desire to become notable artists: "Younger men who in a year or two, or three or five, or ten or twenty, were bound to make their mark, and perhaps follow in the footsteps of the master; others as conspicuously singled out for failure and future mischance—for the hospital, the garret, the river, the Morgue, or worse, the traveller's bag, the road, or even the paternal counter." "Lords of misrule," as Du Maurier calls them, the body of students were comprised of "wits, butts, bullies; the idle and industrious apprentice, the good and the bad, the clean and the dirty (especially the latter)." Still, they were all united and animated by a certain *esprit de corps* and were "working very happily and genially together, on the whole, and always willing to help each other with sincere artistic council if it was asked for seriously, though it was not always couched in terms very flattering to one's self-love."[15]

During his year with Gleyre, George lived with his mother and sister, rather than in his studio. One gets the impression from *Trilby*, however, that he might have lived the life of a true bohemian, as did many of the French students in the Latin Quarter. George actually retained his solid, middle-class values, even though some of his friends adopted a very unconventional style of life. Most of George's friends, in fact, were British and included among the art students such men as Thomas Lamont, Thomas Armstrong, Edward Poynter, and the American James Whistler. Lamont later went on to become a reputable minor painter who specialized in Spanish scenes. Armstrong became a much better known artist who exhibited landscape and figure pieces at the Royal Academy and Grosvenor Gallery. He spent the latter part of his life as art director of South Kensington Museum. Poynter's oil paintings, such as *Israel in Egypt* and *Atalanta's Race*, were to win him an international reputation. He later became president of the Royal Academy. Whistler was the greatest painter of the group and is best known for his *Arrangement in Grey and Black No. 1: The Artist's Mother* and *Symphony in White No. 1: The White Girl*.

Over thirty years after Du Maurier left his art studies in Paris, when he was writing *Trilby*, he used these four artists as models for his characters "The Laird" (Lamont), Taffy (Armstrong), Lorrimer (Poynter), and Joe Sibley (Whistler).

Antwerp, Malines, Dusseldorf

After a year in Paris, George unexplainably left for Antwerp in the summer of 1857. His year in Paris proved to be more important to his psychological than to his artistic development. Ormond notes that his year in France reinforced his Englishness: "It is worth asking how French Du Maurier really was, when one considers how few French friends he made, and how profoundly English in attitude he remained." She then points to the curious paradox that "Du Maurier's disenchantment with the French way of life and temperament coincided with his happy year as an art student in Paris. The memory of his Passy childhood remained untarnished, but a marked dislike of the French race soon became evident."[16]

In a letter to his friend Tom Armstrong in 1862 Du Maurier enclosed a cartoon entitled "The Two Voices" that depicts the English and French elements in his character arguing with each other. The English self is boisterously moralistic and, like an exorcist, attempts to cast out the French fiend: "I know you thoroughly! You would stick to me closer than ever, and taunt me with my weakness. No, no! fiend! You are getting weaker and weaker. I revel in my power over you!" The bold and jaunty French self, which complains because the English self keeps him from kissing everybody, finally exits "in a frightful funk."[17] A playful self-parody that takes its title from Tennyson's somber poem, the cartoon nevertheless illustrates Du Maurier's vivid sense of his split personality and foreshadows the theme of duality that runs through all of his novels. The cartoon also illustrates the dominance of the English over the French element in his character, a relationship that appears to be biographically accurate.

George continued his art studies in Belgium by enrolling in the Antwerp Academy of Fine Arts, directed by the historical painter Nicaise de Keyser. There he became an intimate friend with Felix

Moscheles, a bohemian character whose father was a famous pianist. Like Svengali, Du Maurier's famous character in *Trilby*, Moscheles had Semitic features, a love of music, and the newly discovered power of mesmerism. He and Du Maurier turned the weeks into one prolonged holiday, drinking, smoking, singing, and, in general, indulging their youthful sense of freedom.

Du Maurier enjoyed only two months of these carefree, bohemian days before he experienced the greatest shock of his life: twenty-three years old, he suddenly lost the sight in his left eye, and with it his hopes of ever becoming a painter. He describes the horrific moment:

I was drawing from a model, when suddenly the girl's head seemed to me to dwindle to the size of a walnut. I clapped my hand over my left eye. Had I been mistaken? I could see as well as ever. But when in its turn I covered my right eye, I learned what had happened. My left eye had failed me; it might be altogether lost. It was so sudden a blow that I was as thunderstruck.[18]

It appears that he suffered a detached retina, but the medical advice he received over the next few months proved to be devastating in its inaccuracy. Du Maurier consulted a famous Jesuit oculist who assured him that the blindness was temporary and could be cured by rest. He and his mother moved to Malines, a quiet town full of abbeys and seminaries, in hopes of restoring his sight.

Moscheles, meanwhile, continued to visit Du Maurier and his lively antics and moral support helped to lessen Du Maurier's great anxiety about his vision. Together they would stroll the streets looking for attractive girls, and one of their searches proved to be providential. Octavie, a seventeen-year-old girl who worked in a tobacco shop, became the object of their affections. Carry, as they called her, seemed, in Moscheles's words: "to be born with the intuitive knowledge that there was only one life worth living, that of the Bohemian, and to be at the same time well protected by a pretty reluctance to admit as much."[19] Ormond believes that Carry had become Du Maurier's mistress. He began writing a novel about her, *Les Noces de Picciola*, and did a series of drawings that showed him, Moscheles, and Carry in a menage à trois. Ormond offers no proof, however, to support her conjecture. Indeed, the novel and drawings may simply reveal Du Maurier's sexual fantasies and nothing more.[20] But more important, Carry served as the model for the character of Trilby, the charming grisette, who would soon become known across England and America.

Despite the pleasant interlude with Carry, Du Maurier was still profoundly, if quietly, depressed over the loss of his sight. His condition decidedly was not improving with rest. He consulted another specialist, this time a professor at the University of Ghent, who told him that the Louvain physician was incompetent and that he could effect a cure. The treatment, of course, failed and Du Maurier was again crushed. He returned to the first specialist fearing he might lose the sight of both eyes, since the right one was now causing him discomfort. His interview with the Jesuit oculist is chillingly recorded:

"You seem a courageous young man, and I may tell you that one day when I told a young man what I am going to tell you, he blew his brains out at my door. *Your other eye is going*, and I advise you to seek some employment in which eyesight will not be much needed." He (the oculist) then made evident signs that the interview was ended, took his fee, and pulled off his skull cap to bow him out.[21]

In despair, Du Maurier returned to the professor at Ghent, who reassured him that he could save his right eye, if not the left. Whom to believe? He finally sought a third opinion from a well-known German oculist, Hofrathe de Leeuwe, near Dusseldorf. It was 1859, almost two years after he first lost his sight, when Du Maurier finally received a substantial prognosis: he would never again see out of his left eye, de Leeuwe told him, but with reasonable care he need not fear ever losing the sight of his right eye. His spirits began to pick up and, indeed, his right eye no longer felt the initial strain that caused him so much concern.

While in Dusseldorf Du Maurier began brief romances with two young ladies. One was with a mysterious figure nicknamed "Damask" who was dying of consumption. The other was Louisa Lewis, a friend of his sister Isabella. His flirtations were cut short, however, when the Wightwick family arrived on a holiday excursion, for

Emma, now grown into a beautiful, dark-haired young woman, immediately captured all of Du Maurier's attention. Three years later they would be married.

But first Du Maurier had to find some way to make a living. Now twenty-six years old, in love, and reassured about his sight, he began to regain his hope for a career in art. Paging through a copy of *Punch*, he was fascinated by the quality of John Leech's drawings. They reminded him that illustration need not be hack work but could be a true form of art. Accepting the fact that he could no longer become a painter, Du Maurier looked toward the possibility of becoming a famous illustrator in London, and in May of 1860, he left Dusseldorf with high hopes of accomplishing that goal.

London

In the summer of 1860 he began making the rounds of various magazines in London seeking employment as an illustrator. He was particularly eager to be accepted by one of the three most distinguished illustrated magazines of the day, *Cornhill*, *Once A Week*, and *Punch*. He finally got a set of drawings published in *Once A Week* in the fall of 1860. They were illustrations for a story entitled "Faristan and Fatima." Although very mediocre works, they showed enough promise to interest the magazine in printing his drawings on a regular basis.

In October of 1860 Mark Lemon, the editor of *Punch*, published Du Maurier's first cartoon in that magazine. The young artist's dream of having his work appear in the company of England's finest cartoonists had finally come true. It was a crudely drawn satire of the current fad for photography that showed himself, Whistler, and Lamont entering a photographer's studio. Both Lamont and Du Maurier are holding cigarettes, the latter speaking as Dick Tinto:

PHOTOGRAPHER:	"No smoking here, sir!"
DICK TINTO:	"Oh! A thousand pardons! I was not aware that ———"
PHOTOGRAPHER:	(interrupting, with dignified severity): "Please to remember, gentlemen, that this is not a *Common Hartist's* studio!"

Du Maurier wrote his mother full accounts of his days in London—and the adventures he made them seem. Desperate to succeed in his new world and full of youthful bravado, he made it appear that all of London society was at his feet. The truth of the matter is that it took him several years of hard work and frustration to begin to make a name for himself. Frequently he was very lonely and disappointed. He kept up a brave front, however, as evidenced in this passage from a letter he wrote to his mother in January of 1861: "I have already gone to work again hard, and you know how I work when I'm at it—forget to wash, to eat, even to smoke, and the result amply repays me for today I sent to *Once A Week* a little bedside scene, which will make an effect. Everybody has brought out bedside scenes, Millais two within the last six months, and I make bold to say that mine if well engraved will smash them all."[22]

Like his grandfather, Du Maurier was eager to be associated with the upper classes. Although he continued to cultivate the friendship or acquaintance with numerous artists, including Whistler, Poynter, and the *Punch* artist, Charles Keene, he took especial pains to be invited to the homes of aristocrats, such as Alexander Ionides, a wealthy Greek merchant, who introduced Du Maurier to a world of unconventional, beautiful, intellectual, and cosmopolitan people. The evenings he spent at Tulse Hill, the Ionides estate, included cultivated conversation, amateur theatricals, singing and music, and the company of beautiful tall women who would later reappear in Du Maurier's drawings.

Du Maurier also spent much time at Little Holland House, the home of the snobbish and well-to-do Val Princep family. The Princeps collected famous artists and writers with a frightening vigor. Holman Hunt, John Millais, Dante Gabriel Rossetti, Alfred Tennyson, Robert Browning, and William Makepeace Thackeray were among those whom the family lionized, although Du Maurier did not happen to see any of these people on the occasions he was invited. After an evening at Little Holland House, he wrote this account to his mother:

I must tell you about the Princeps. There were three beautiful women, sisters, who married 1. Col. Dalrymple, 2. Lord Somers, 3. Mr. Princep, a

great East Indian of immense wealth I'm told. These 3 women stick
together, and have formed a sort of nucleus, round which gather all that
there is of swell; the nobilitee, the gentree, the litherathure, polithics and art
of the counthree, by jasus! It is a nest of proeraphaelites, where Hunt,
Millais, Rossetti, Watts, Leighton etc., Tennyson, the Brownings and
Thackeray etc. and tutti quanti receive dinners and incense, and cups of tea
handed to them by these women almost kneeling.[23]

Meanwhile Du Maurier's love affair with Emma Wightwick continued to develop despite the fact that his mother was strongly urging
him to marry a wealthy heiress. In 1861 he proposed marriage to
Emma, and, in an attempt to offset his mother's displeasure, he wrote
her a letter in which he depicts Emma as his guardian angel: "I really
can't tell you how enormously and preposterously I adore the fair
Emma, and how her influence on me is wholesome; good in every
way; had it not been for her I should have yielded to the seduction of society and other seductions much more dangerous (in Society)
—perfect ruin to an artist like me."[24] Still, he did not feel financially
secure enough for marriage despite the gradual increase in acceptance
of his drawings by other magazines. Eventually *Once A Week* began
offering him enough serials to illustrate that he felt he could go ahead
with his plans, and on January 3, 1863, he and Emma were married.
This was the first time in his life that he openly defied his mother's
wishes. Although she eventually came to accept his decision and to
enjoy the company of Emma, Du Maurier never forgot the anguish
experienced in asserting his independence. Years later in *The Martian*
the scenario is replayed when the hero, Barty Josselin, must choose
between a wealthy, aristocratic blonde named Julia Royce and a poor,
dark-haired Jew named Leah Gibson.

Settling down after a honeymoon in Boulogne, Du Maurier began
to place his work in the prestigious *Cornhill*, *Leisure Hour*, and *London
Society*, and his contributions to *Once A Week* showed continued improvement. Conscious of his failure to become a painter, he still held
fast to the highest artistic standards: "I want to reach the utmost
perfection that my talent is susceptible of, and get to that point that
everything I attempt should turn out a complete and perfect work of
art."[25] He did not later always live up to the high standard he set for

himself, however, especially during his later years on *Punch* when, working on too many projects at the same time, he quickly turned out drawings according to ready-made formulas.

His financial liabilities gradually lessened but his family responsibilities grew when Emma gave birth to a daughter, Beatrix, named after Thackeray's heroine, in 1864, and a son, Guy Louis, the following year. Unlike his father, Du Maurier was a devoted parent who lavished a great deal of attention upon his children. Not only did he spend many hours with them at home but later, when they began to grow up, he took them on many family excursions in England and France. He also combined work with domestic pleasure by having his children later model for many of his drawings for *Punch*.

John Leech, *Punch*'s foremost illustrator since its earliest days, died in 1864 and the editor, Mark Lemon, called a meeting in November to consider his successor. Charles Keene and John Tenniel both recommended Du Maurier for the position. A few days later he elatedly joined the staff of England's most successful and influential magazine, in whose pages he would mature into one of the most skillful illustrators of the period. In January, 1865, two months after his appointment, Du Maurier wrote his mother: "I am regularly on the staff of Punch now which is a very good thing besides being a very pleasant one; and I've no doubt that when I get into the reins, in a few months or so, they will find DM a very useful person, and pay him accordingly."[26]

It took a while for Du Maurier to discover his role in *Punch*. Leech had focused his work on politics, sports, and low life. Tenniel, however, came to specialize in the full-page political drawings. Charles Keene covered scenes of low life. Lemon thus instructed Du Maurier not to try to be broadly funny, but to be light and graceful, and deal with the gentler aspects of English life. This proved to be the exact role for which Du Maurier's temperament and interest suited him, and within a few years his talent blossomed and his reputation as the best pictorial satirist of the upper classes was firmly established.

In 1866 Du Maurier contributed his first major work to *Punch*, "A Legend of Camelot." It was a series of drawings that satirized the romantic cult that affected the style of Dante Gabriel Rossetti, and it anticipated his later attack on the pretensions of the aesthetes. His work load for the magazine, meanwhile, soon settled at two cartoons a week, a large and a small one, but the quality of his drawings was uneven. Some of his pieces were brilliant in both their arrangement of figures and their satirical tone but others were done with little enthusiasm. As Ormond points out, "All his life he tended to work unevenly, long bouts of idleness alternating with sudden bursts of activity."[27]

Besides his work for *Punch* and the other magazines, Du Maurier illustrated a great many books, including novels of the popular writer Elizabeth Gaskell: *Cranford* (1864); *Lizzie Leigh*, *The Grey Woman*, and *Cousin Phillis* (one volume, 1865); *North and South* and *A Dark Night's Work* (both in 1867). In 1868 he was commissioned to illustrate Thackeray's *Henry Esmond*, a task he especially welcomed since Thackeray was his favorite author. Other volumes he illustrated during this period include Richard Barham's *The Ingoldsby Legends* (1866), Douglas Jerrold's *The Story of a Feather* (1867), and Owen Meredith's *Lucile* (1868). Most of these illustrations are competent and pleasant supplements to the texts but some of them, as in *The Story of a Feather* and *The Ingoldsby Legends*, are superior works of art in themselves.

The increasing demands upon Du Maurier during the 1860s intensified his hypochondria. His eye began to bother him again and thinking his habit of cigarette smoking was the cause, he cut down to five cigarettes a day. His family, meanwhile, continued to grow when Sylvia Jocelyn was born in 1866 and Marie Louise in 1868. With four children now, and uneasy in the heart of London, the Du Mauriers moved from their lodgings in Great Russell Street to Kensington, which provided them a little more privacy and seclusion.

Hampstead

But Du Maurier really was seeking the remembered atmosphere of his childhood in Passy and finally found such a pastoral retreat in Hampstead, to which he moved his family in the summer of 1869. Although close to London and the *Punch* office, Hampstead was a country village on the north side of the Thames Valley. It was a favorite location for landscape painters, from Constable to Ford

Madox Brown, and its quiet charm provided many subjects for Du Maurier's drawings in *Punch*. Most of the residents in the area were wealthy and cultivated and Du Maurier soon became involved in Hampstead's rich social life. Their new neighborly acquaintances now included the poet, William Allingham, the novelist, Sir Walter Besant, and fellow artist, Kate Greenaway. In this setting the Du Mauriers' fifth and last child, Gerald, was born in March, 1873.

The annual summer holiday for the family had an important influence upon Du Maurier's *Punch* cartoons, which exhibit scenes from his travels to Dieppe, Le Havre, and Étretat. Chang, the family's St. Bernard, was an inseparable companion on these trips and his size created enormous problems. In a letter to Armstrong in 1877 Du Maurier writes:

I cannot describe all the trouble Chang has been. . . . What fiend induced one to tie such a millstone round my neck! We cannot sit outside a café, or stop at a shop window without a crowd collecting. I have to go thro' all the history of him; at hotels I have to take a bedroom a part, for him to sleep with me; he alternately drinks and snores all night and every time I move he comes and licks me in the dark; at every new place he howls the whole of the first night if alone and the railway journeys are too fearful! . . . If I talk of parting with him there's a general howl all around, let alone my own fondness for the beast and his tyrannical affection for me, which would perhaps kill him if we were to separate.[28]

Readers of *Punch* soon became fond of Chang and, with Du Maurier, were much saddened with his death in 1883.

In 1874 Du Maurier, now forty years old, moved his family to New Grove House, in Hampstead, where they were to live for the next twenty years. Du Maurier's old friends, Armstrong, Lamont, and Poynter, did not visit much any longer and he began a close friendship with the painter, John Millais, and often visited George Eliot and G. H. Lewes. During this period Du Maurier drew most of his characters from models, either hired or chosen from among his family or household staff. Throughout the seventies one may see in *Punch* numerous drawings of his children, and occasionally Emma and the family dog, set against the manicured, though rustic, Hampstead background. Many of these idyllic drawings, with their close family groupings, are reminiscent of the scenes in Passy that Du Maurier later illustrated in *Peter Ibbetson*.

Once again Du Maurier's good eye started to trouble him. It began to cloud over and between 1872 and 1874 he lived with the prospect of going totally blind. His doctor told him that he could continue his drawings provided they were done on a larger scale so as to avoid eye strain. Not only did this advice cause the engraver trouble, for he had to reduce the larger drawing by photographic process before the blocks were made, but the quality of Du Maurier's work deteriorated. He simply could not adjust to the greater scale, and disappointed with himself, he reverted to old themes and formulas for his drawings.

Under the editorship of Tom Taylor, Du Maurier began his cartoon series on the aesthetes. For about ten years, from 1875 to 1885, the cult of beauty was a prominent London phenomenon. Authors such as Théophile Gautier, Charles Baudelaire, Dante Gabriel Rossetti, and Walter Pater set forth the philosophy of the aesthetic movement, and it was only a matter of time before it became faddish for second-rate minds to attempt to embody it. Du Maurier's satiric drawings appeared over nine years, from 1873 to 1882, during which time he created a set of memorable aesthetes: Mrs. Cimabue Brown (an aesthetic Philistine), Jellaby Postlethwaite (an aesthete poet), Maudle (an Oscar Wilde type), Prigsby (a hanger-on), Peter Pilcox (a sculptor), Grigsby (an ordinary man who attempts to follow the aesthetic fashion), Mrs. Ponsonby de Tomkyns and Sir Gorgius Midas (the nouveaux riches and patrons of the arts). The creation of these recurrent and vivid characters, along with the elaborate dialogue that Du Maurier wrote for them, revealed a talent that would later find a fuller expression in his career as a novelist.

Ormond suggests that the aesthetic cartoons reveal Du Maurier's distrust of Whistler and Rossetti, whose bohemian values he had long since dropped in favor of a comfortable middle-class family life and social standing. She goes on to say that the cartoons also reveal Du Maurier's snobbery: "His treatment of the rise of the professional classes and the *nouveaux riches*, as typified by Mrs. Ponsonby de Tomkyns and Sir Gorguis Midas, reveals his essential snobbery, conservatism and loathing of change."[29] As he grew older he became more snobbish, more conservative, and more distressed by the continual changes he saw all around him. His snobbery led him to preach the benefits of human eugenics in *The Martian*, and all three of his novels call upon dreams or memories as the means by which one can escape the vulgarity of the present and find fulfillment in a beautiful imagined past.

Du Maurier's social cartoons for *Punch* during the 1870s were characterized by his beautiful, tall, aristocratic women. He may well have made the tall woman fashionable, and some observers declare that he permanently raised the height of the average English girl by several inches. His gentlemen were also very tall, slim, and elegant. For the most part his ugly people were small. As Henry James observed, "The world was, very simply, divided for him into what was beautiful and what was ugly, and especially into what *looked so*."[30] Even his dog Chang had to be tall! His fascination with tall, beautiful creatures derived, in part, from the fact that Du Maurier himself was so short. Also, he believed that beauty of character was reflected in one's statuesque physique. To be magnanimous and virile, one had to be like his hero in *The Martian*, Barty Josselin—over six feet tall, handsome, and powerful.

In any event, most of his social cartoons were drawn to reinforce a dialogue or elaborate caption beneath them. Practically none of the drawings, like modern cartoons, is humorous in itself. Among his favorite subjects were foolish clergymen, pompous gentlemen, flirtatious young ladies, and insufferable singers and musicians. Interspersed among the social satires were drawings of his family that had a strong sentimental appeal. Although he did a few cartoons about low life, the fact of the matter was that he knew practically nothing about the lower classes—he avoided them insofar as was possible and he willingly left the subject to Charles Keene.

Upon Tom Taylor's death in 1880, Frank Burnand became editor of *Punch*. Disappointed that he was not chosen for the post, Du Maurier, now forty-six years old, took a less active interest in the magazine, though he continued to supply drawings for many years to come. Du Maurier's sense of his own importance to *Punch* was badly misconceived. His real value to the magazine was to be the chief satirist of the upper classes and in that role, so clearly designed for him years earlier by Mark Lemon, he consistently provided an elegance of tone and line that matched perfectly, by contrast, the bold and comic earthiness of Charles Keene's drawings. Du Maurier was out of touch with the common man and was too limited in his perception of English society to have made a good editor. But he never really saw this about himself and felt that his years of service on the magazine qualified him to be editor. His pride was hurt and the drawings he submitted during the 1880s were lacking in freshness, often reverting to the groupings and humor he pioneered twenty years earlier.

Financial problems at this time led him to seek work with book publishers and with other magazines besides *Punch*. He began to fragment his talent and energy as he moved from one job to another. The *Cornhill* printed many of his works until 1886 when it ceased using illustrations. He was also illustrating a number of undistinguished books, with the one important exception being Henry James's *Washington Square* (1880). That work brought about a close friendship with James, who had long admired Du Maurier's perceptive and comic depiction of London high society. Had Du Maurier been made editor of *Punch*, he might never have illustrated James's novel and developed the author's friendship which, providentially, brought a unity and focus to Du Maurier's life that led to his fame as a novelist.

Although James first met Du Maurier in the late 1870s, it was not until the 1880s that their friendship developed. In 1882 James visited Du Maurier in order to prepare an article about him for *Century Magazine*. James's fondness and respect for Du Maurier can be traced in their correspondence and in the three essays that James wrote about him. As Ormond has noted, James was not only a good friend, but "he liberated Du Maurier's long-unused intellect."[31] He sent him numerous books, set up a reading program for him, and engaged him in complex discussions of French literature.

Each man was able to help the other not only as companions but as writers. Du Maurier, for example, gave James the idea for his famous short story "The Real Thing." The artist William Frith had once sent two members of "society" to serve as models for Du Maurier. Down on their luck, the shabby genteel couple simply lacked the ability to pose and were useless to the artist. James happily used this situation in his story to dramatize the gulf between art and life.

Du Maurier also offered James the story line of *Trilby*. This time, however, James urged Du Maurier to try his own hand at writing a novel. James's insistence so stirred Du Maurier that the next evening, in a burst of creativity, he wrote the first part of *Peter Ibbetson*. There is no satisfactory explanation for why he did not begin the *Trilby* story. Du Maurier himself simply records: "But that night after going home it occurred to me that it would be worthwhile trying to write, after all. So on the impulse I sat down and began to work. It was not on 'Trilby,' however, but on 'Peter Ibbetson.' "[32] It may be that James's rejection of the *Trilby* plot, combined with the fact that Du Maurier was still an untested author, led to his writing about a subject that obsessed him and which he knew best—his childhood in Passy. It may also be that in his first novel Du Maurier did not want to challenge conventional prudery with the story of a young girl who was sexually liberated. In any event, at the age of fifty-five Du Maurier amazed his family, friends, and literary gossips when he began a new career as a novelist, introducing the world to his private fantasies of youth, dreams, and romantic love.

By the summer of 1889 he had completed the first version of *Peter Ibbetson*. His friends, including Henry James, urged him to publish it, and in 1890 Du Maurier sent to the American magazine, *Harper's Monthly*, where it appeared, illustrated by the author, between June and September of 1891. That same year it came out in a two-volume book edition without illustrations, and then in a one-volume edition, with the author's illustrations published by a subsidiary of Harper's. The book sold a modest number of copies and the critical reception was unenthusiastic, but its popularity grew by leaps and bounds after the publication of his enormously successful second novel.

Early in 1892 Du Maurier began work on *Trilby*. The story line was the same one that he offered James earlier: a foreign Jew mesmerizes a grisette with no musical talent and turns her into a singer who wins international fame. Fearing for his sight, Du Maurier worked quickly and completed the novel in about ten months. Harper's accepted the manuscript and Du Maurier began work on the illustrations. The first installment was published in January, 1894, in *Harper's Monthly Magazine*, and it met with immediate success. The March issue, however, inadvertently set off an explosive response in England. Du Maurier's satiric portrait of his old friend James Whistler as "the idle apprentice" and egotistical "king of Bohemia," Joe Sibley, enraged the feisty artist. Somehow he acquired a copy of the third installment of *Trilby*, published in March, and two months later wrote a fiery counterattack in the *Pall Mall Gazette* accusing Du Maurier of viciously betraying their friendship: "Now that my back is turned, the old *marmite* of our *pot-au-feu* he fills with the picric acid of thirty years' spite, and, in an American Magazine, fires off his bomb of mendacious recollection and poisoned rancune."[33] A reporter for the *Pall Mall Gazette* then obtained an interview with Du Maurier to get his response to Whistler's letter. Published the following week, the interview set forth Du Maurier's defense of his position along with an important admission that "in the character of Joe Sibley . . . I have drawn certain lines with Mr. Whistler in my mind."[34] Whistler took this remark as Du Maurier's admission of guilt and began a campaign to force him to apologize and to withdraw the character of Joe Sibley from the book edition of the novel. Du Maurier wrote his publisher indicating his desire "to replace the character of 'Joe Sibley' by another (& better one)."[35] Meanwhile, however, Whistler had begun the legal process for a libel suit.

Over the following months Whistler became obsessed with the subject and began to imagine that a sinister plot was being developed to ruin his career. His lawyer wrote to Harper's demanding that Du Maurier's work containing the libel be stopped, that the March number of the magazine be destroyed, and that a satisfactory apology be published in the magazine. The legal entanglements and correspondence continued to grow at an alarming pace. Harper's was clearly on the defensive and offered to meet many of Whistler's initial demands but Whistler, who had a reputation for being litigious, was beginning to enjoy the combat and hoped to stop the publication of *Trilby* entirely. His early irascibility had by now developed into a personal vendetta against Du Maurier.

Du Maurier replaced the character of Joe Sibley in the book edition of *Trilby* with Bald Anthony, a character partly drawn after the Swiss painter, Huniker, with whom Du Maurier shared a studio in Dusseldorf. Harper's agreed to suppress the illustration entitled "The Two Apprentices" that depicted a clearly recognizable Whistler dressed like a peacock, sporting a jaunty cane, bows on his shoes, a flower in his lapel, and a broad-brimmed hat with a flying ribbon—in short, the figure of a ridiculous aesthete. Harper's also agreed to stop future sales of the March issue of the European edition of its magazine and to publish a letter of apology in the September number. The publisher refused, however, to cancel the sales of the March issue in America or to print an apology in its American number.

Whistler greatly enjoyed his triumph but neither Harper's nor Du Maurier was much disturbed by the quarrel or its settlement. *Trilby* was well on its way toward becoming an all-time best-seller and Whistler's public furor simply increased the sales of both magazine and book versions of the novel. Furthermore, despite the minor surgery that Du Maurier performed on the character of Joe Sibley, everyone could recognize a number of Whistler's traits and mannerisms in the character of Bald Anthony. The end result of the hullabaloo raised by Whistler over his portrayal in *Trilby* was to increase the sales and popularity of the novel.

The book edition quickly became a best-seller in both England and America. Readers were intensely interested in the unfamiliar world of the Latin Quarter, the strange bohemian characters, and the strong romantic plot. The *Trilby* boom was on and commercial interests attempted to exploit it with Trilby parties, Trilby shoes, and even Trilby sweets and lozenges. The word "trilby" itself has now entered the English language as the name of a soft felt hat with an indented crown, after the hat worn by Little Billee in some of Du Maurier's illustrations and in the London play version of the novel. Herbert Beerbohm Tree produced the play by Paul Potter at the Haymarket Theatre, where it was an enormous success. Tree played Svengali, Dorothea Baird played Trilby, H. B. Irving was Little Billee, and Gerald Du Maurier (then aged twenty-two) took the part of Zouzou, the French dragoon.

Tired and still troubled by his health, Du Maurier felt that his fame arrived too late and consequently it did little to raise his flagging spirits. He gradually became more comfortable with his success and late in 1894 began work on his third novel, a romantic fantasy entitled *The Martian*. It is the story of a man whose mind becomes possessed by a female spirit from Mars. She turns him into a famous author and finally is reincarnated as his daughter. He completed the work only a short time before his death in 1896. He took more pains with the writing of his last novel than he did with the earlier ones and considered it his best work. As James notes: "The other books had come and gone—so far as execution was concerned—in a flash. . . . To his latest novel, on the other hand, he gave his greatest care: it was a labour of many months, and he went over it again and again. There is nothing indeed that, as the light faded, he did not more intensely go over."[36]

The first part appeared in *Harper's Monthly Magazine* for the month in which Du Maurier died. When published in London in 1898 neither the critics nor the public much liked it. As a work of art it is the least successful of his novels, but is rich in autobiographical detail. It may be that he regarded it as his best work because he put so much time into it. It is not clear why the public did not concur. After all, if they rushed out to buy *Trilby* in order to discover the strange world of bohemia and hypnotism, one would think they might be interested in the subject of reincarnation, life on Mars, and automatic writing.

After many happy years at Hampstead, Du Maurier and his wife moved to Oxford Square, near New Hyde Park, in 1895. It is uncertain why he moved, since he always loved Hampstead and despised Oxford Square. Ormond suggests that he had grown weary of life and that the move "was almost the expression of a death wish."[37] His health steadily declined in his new quarters and on October 7, 1896, at the age of sixty-two, he died of what appears to have been congestive heart failure. His funeral at the Hampstead Parish Church was attended by numerous distinguished artists and writers, including the *Punch* staff, his old friends Armstrong, Lamont, and Poynter, and Henry James.

His ashes were deposited in Hampstead cemetery, near his former residence. On the panel erected to his memory are inscribed the last two lines of *Trilby*, being the final couplet of his translation of Léon Monte-Naken's "Peu de chose":

> A little trust that when we die
> We reap our sowing. And so—good bye!

THE SIX-MARK TEA-POT

Aesthetic Bridegroom: "It is quite consummate, is it not?"

Intense Bride: "It is, indeed! Oh, Algernon, let us live up to it!" *Punch,* 1880.

Chapter Two
The Artist

The Novelist's Eye

Toward the end of his career as an artist-illustrator Du Maurier expressed the rather daring opinion that the illustrator in black-and-white may be as important as the novelist or painter—provided he "illustrate life from [his] *own* point of view . . . (as the social artists of *Punch* have done from the beginning)." If he has done his work well, he argues, and has "faithfully represented the life of his time— he has perpetuated what he has seen with his own bodily eyes . . . his unpretending little sketches may, perhaps, have more interest for those who come across them in another hundred years, than many an ambitious historical or classical canvas."[1] In rendering the characters and social details of his day, the illustrator "may still have the power to charm and amuse" later generations by the mere virtue of the "literal truth" that resides in his drawings.

Although he illustrated numerous books, Du Maurier believed that the pages of *Punch* afforded him the proper medium in which to develop his drawings into an art form that was as autonomous and enduring as an oil painting or a novel. The cartoon provided him this autonomy, for it was independent of the surrounding text. As an illustrator of books he was keenly aware of the subservient role of the artist whose duty was to portray someone else's characters and scenes. "If authors would learn a little how to draw themselves," he writes, "they would not put such difficulties in the artist's way, and expect the impossible of him, such as that he should draw three sides of a house in one picture, or show the heroine's full face, tearstained, as she gazes on her lover vanishing in the middle of the background."[2] Despite some striking illustrations he did for the novels of Mrs. Gaskell, Douglas Jerrold, and Thackeray, Du Maurier's artistic talent flourished in the more congenial atmosphere of *Punch*. No longer restricted by an author's conception of character and scene, Du Maurier was faced with the awesome task of drawing directly from life and reproducing what he saw there in a structured and meaningful way. He was helped in this endeavor by the organization of the magazine itself, which had on hand artists who had staked out their special areas, including the lower classes of society, sporting events, and politics. As Du Maurier put it, "I have generally stuck to the 'classes' because C. K. [Charles Keene] seems to have monopolized the 'masses.' "[3]

After doing a number of random drawings, initial letters, and literary parodies, Du Maurier began to develop a pattern and structure for his cartoons in *Punch* that gave them a life of their own. Between the late 1860s and the end of the 1880s he created a fictional world as complex and self-contained as many a novel. As Henry James put it, "*Punch* had never before suspected that it was so artistic; had never taken itself, in such matters, so seriously."[4] An avid reader as well as prodigious illustrator of fiction and a great admirer of Thackeray, Meredith, Henry James, and Mrs. Gaskell, Du Maurier produced work in *Punch* that was strongly influenced by the form of the novel. The editor of *Punch* gave him his subject—the upper classes—and the novel provided him a structure for rendering that subject. The fact that late in life he turned to writing novels is really not surprising when one considers his thirty years of work in *Punch* not only as an artistic end in itself but as his lengthy apprenticeship to becoming a novelist. The relationship between Du Maurier the artist and Du Maurier the novelist is an intimate one.

Henry James was the first person to observe the similarity between Du Maurier's drawings and the English novel of manners. Writing about the illustrations in the *Cornhill* he says that Du Maurier

has reproduced every possible situation that is likely to be encountered in the English novel of manners; he has interpreted pictorially innumerable flirtations, wooings, philanderings, raptures. The interest of the English novel of manners is frequently the interest of the usual; the situations presented to the artist are apt to lack superficial strangeness. A lady and gentleman sitting in a drawing-room, a lady and a gentleman going out to walk, a sad young woman watching at a sick-bed, a handsome young man lighting a ciga-

A Little Christmas Dream, *Punch*, 1868.

rette. . . . In these drawing-room and flower-garden episodes the artist is
thoroughly at home.[5]

James goes on to say that Du Maurier's cartoons in *Punch* remind him
of the fashionable novel that flourished in the 1830s, and if it were to
be revised Du Maurier would be the man to do the pictures: "the
pictures of people rather slim and still, with long necks and limbs so
straight that they look stiff, who might be treated with the amount of
decision justified . . . by their passion for talking bad French."
James draws still another parallel between the drawings and literature:
"he has made 'society' completely his own—he has sounded its
depths, explored its mysteries, discovered and divulged its secrets.
His observations of these things is extraordinarily acute, and his
illustrations, taken together, form a complete comedy of manners."[6]
Like George Meredith and Henry James, Du Maurier preferred
persons that, in the words of Meredith's Mountstuart Jenkinson,
"shone in the sun."[7] And like them he was more concerned with the
subtleties of the comic spirit rather than with the vulgarity of boisterous laughter. It is in the setting of the Victorian drawing room and,
more finely, in the mid-region between two people in conversation
where false constructions are put by either party upon what is said that
Du Maurier, like the novelists, perceived the source of comedy was to
be found. The drawing room belonged to an age that was willing to
sacrifice much for the sake of appearances: illusion became the only
reality. It was like a stage in which elegantly costumed people, set
against carefully arranged furniture and draperies, acted out their
lives according to the rigid script of good manners. Against this
artificial setting, manners were destined to be false, and good manners became almost synonymous with insincerity.
Du Maurier's public world is essentially restricted to the drawing
room, the after-dinner entertainments, the alcove looking out to the
drawing room, or the dinner table—high society trying its best to be
highly civilized. Unlike Thomas Hardy and Charles Dickens, Du
Maurier showed little interest in the outer world of highways or
rugged heaths. When he does depict outdoor scenes they are usually
of manicured lawns, tennis matches, or the artful landscaped area of
Hampstead where he lived.

The characters that Du Maurier created to inhabit and visit the elegant rooms of his cartoons also suggest the novelist's eye. As a comedy of manners, the panoramic world of his cartoons contained hundreds of different characters and character types, from foolish Frenchmen to ridiculous clergymen. The features and dress of a character may vary from cartoon to cartoon but the type remains essentially the same. What gives some of Du Maurier's characters a novelistic turn, however, is that he created a set of specific characters who appeared many times over the years. Serial publication was the common form used for fiction during this period. Figures such as Mrs. Cimabue Brown, Jellaby Postlethwaite, Maudle, Mrs. Ponsonby De Tomkyns, and Sir Gorgius Midas became popular attractions that gave a unity to the cartoons in much the same way that the Pickwickians did for the monthly parts of Dickens's picaresque novel. The characters usually do not develop and grow but the reader is delighted to hear and see more of their sayings and doings in each new issue of the magazine. Gradually their reappearance invests them with a life of their own.

Having established a world of artifice where style makes both the man and the woman, and having created an array of characters, Du Maurier assumed the novelist's role again by endowing his people with speech. He wrote his own captions for the cartoons, and these captions are basically of two kinds: the conversational passage—usually a dialogue, or the more elaborate third-person observation by the artist himself. The thousands of lines of dialogue and narration that Du Maurier wrote over the years provided him invaluable practice for the novels he was to write later. In fact, the dialogue under the cartoons is occasionally more succinct and dramatic than that in his novels.

The drawings are seldom humorous in themselves. His stately and beautiful people could be saying practically anything; the captions are therefore necessary to explain the situation and to trigger the humor. Rarely the joker, Du Maurier sought in his captions to elicit from his reader a knowing smile, rather than a laugh. The modern reader, on the other hand, is accustomed to cartoons that are drawn to be humorous in themselves or which depend on a short comic punch line. A person nowadays brings different expectations to a cartoon and consequently may at first be disappointed with Du Maurier's work. Amusing, perhaps, but few real laughs. His cartoons are best viewed and read with the expectation one brings to the novels of Jane Austen, Trollope, or Thackeray. Temperamentally and artistically, Du Maurier belongs with the cast of novelists who delight in the in-door drama of witty conversation, social maneuverings, the deftly articulated snub, and the artful though oftentimes foolish exhibition of one's sense of superiority.

Consistent with the dualism that has been noted about his life and with the theme of dualism that runs through his three novels, his drawings reveal a similar division, in this case, between his public and private worlds. The greatest number of his drawings depict London's fashionable society, but he also did several cartoons based upon his own family. Tender, sometimes sentimental, they disclose another side of the artist, one seen again in the delightful opening chapters of *Peter Ibbetson*. Obsessed with the past, Du Maurier's Hampstead cartoons suggest a quaint, unchanging beauty unlike anything else in *Punch*. His private world is seen again in the drawings that depict nightmarish figures, grotesque distortions of reality that in a different guise haunt the pages of *Peter Ibbetson* and *Trilby* years later.

Both of these worlds, the public and the private, exhibit Du Maurier's masterful creation of character and dialogue. First to be examined will be the society pictures that feature the aesthetes, the nouveau riche, clergymen, servants, and liberated women. Herein lies an intensely focused world like that of his novels but which, unlike them, is seen through the eyes of a satirist. Second, the drawings based upon his private life will be discussed, and these present a world that is serious, idealistic, and sometimes frightening. The tone of Du Maurier's novels evolves more directly from these later cartoons than from the former, though both sets were influential in the development of his ability as a novelist.

Society Pictures

Du Maurier's famous crusade against the aesthetic movement in England reflected his long-standing dislike of affectation and his distrust of change. These attitudes are revealed in the parody he did for *Punch* in 1866 entitled "A Legend of Camelot." The stylized paintings and bohemian manners of the Pre-Raphaelites disturbed Du Maurier's conservative sensibilities, and in five full-page drawings, accompanied by clever doggerel verse, he set forth a powerful attack upon the excesses of Rossetti, Morris, and Holman Hunt. The story line of the series is a composite of the Arthurian romance, Tennyson's "Lady of Shalott," and Morris's Arthurian poems. The drawings parody the styles of Rossetti and Hunt. Supporting the popular view that the Pre-Raphaelites were effeminate, Du Maurier's cartoons render the knights in absurdly affected poses. In one scene, for example, Sir Gawaine stands in the background with his finger in his mouth. The women are parodies of the long-haired, quasi-medieval beauties of Rossetti and Morris. His heroine, Braunighrindas, for example, has mounds of flowing tresses fuller and longer than her own body. Du Maurier's couplet extends the parody: "O Moshesh! vat a precioush lot / Of beautiful red hair they've got." Her protruding chin and dour expression also caricature the Pre-Raphaelite ideal of beauty: "How much their upper lipsh do pout! / How very much their chins shtick out!"[8] Besides the parodic figures, these drawings reproduce the excessive symbolism, minute detail, and meditative tone of the Pre-Raphaelites.

Satirists are essentially conservative who employ humor to bring to heel those people who stray too far from the accepted norms and traditions of society. When the so-called aesthetic movement began to flourish in England during the 1870s and 1880s, its excesses made it a ready-made target for Du Maurier's satire. This movement was not a clearly defined nor organized one but rather a loose collection of painters and writers, such as Whistler, Wilde, Morris, and Pater, whose work influenced trends in interior decorating, clothing fashions, language, and encouraged the craze of collecting blue-and-white China. Like Pre-Raphaelitism, aestheticism represented a startling departure from conventional patterns of Victorian life. The followers of aestheticism stood out in a crowd: their dress, their speech, and their ideals all marked them as members of an elite group, sensitive, creative, intense, and dedicated to the ideals of beauty, all trying "to burn always with this hard, gem-like flame."[9]

Du Maurier's aesthetic cartoons appeared between 1873 and 1882. The early drawings, such as the Chinamania series, depicting the fad for collecting China, were unified by theme, the later series by recurrent characters. Whistler and Rossetti were largely responsible for initiating the craze. Interested in the exotic, these two famous men quickly became rival collectors, and the established antique dealers in London began stocking their shelves with expensive pieces of blue-and-white China. Although he was eclectic, buying Japanese as well as Chinese pieces, Whistler, like other connoisseurs, was especially fond of the technically brilliant blue and white wares produced during the reign of Louis XIV's Chinese contemporary, K'ang Hsi. Whistler's interest in the Orient was also expressed in his paintings at the time, such as *Rose and Silver*, *Purple and Rose*, and *Variations in Flesh Color and Green*, all of which feature Oriental women and blue-and-white China vases. [10] The press began to cover the trend toward things Oriental, and in May, 1874, Du Maurier produced his first cartoon on the subject. Entitled "The Passion for Old China," [11] it depicts a woman sitting beneath two shelves displaying China plates and vases; holding a teapot in her lap as if it were a baby. Her husband standing beside her says "I think you might *let me* nurse that teapot a little *now*, Margery! You've had it to yourself all *morning*, you know!"

One of the finest cartoons in this series, however, appeared in 1880, entitled "The Six-Mark Tea-Pot." [12] It satirizes both the China craze and the aesthetes who encouraged it. The "intense bride" in the drawing has all of the appearances of the Pre-Raphaelite woman, especially Rossetti's idealized woman: the thick, full hair that covers the forehead, the strong nose, protruding chin, bee-stung lips, and powerful neck. She is dressed in an elaborate dress with puffed sleeves and an intricate pattern of flowers and birds suggestive of a medieval costume. Examining the teapot the "eshtetic bridegroom" says, "It is quite consummate, is it not?" His bride answers, "It is indeed! Oh, Algernon, let us live up to it!" The dialogue here parodies the diction and exclamatory style of the aesthetes, and the name Algernon calls to mind Algernon Swinburne, the notorious poet who associated with the Pre-Raphaelites. The languishing appearance of the bridegroom is reminiscent of Oscar Wilde and his speech suggestive of his exaggerated style. It has not been previously noted but Du Maurier's cartoon may also be a parody of Whistler's oil painting entitled *Purple and Rose: The Lange Lijzen of the Six Marks* (1864). The six marks in the title of both works refer to the potter's marks. The Delft term for the elongated figures, the "long Lizzies," explains the "Lange Lijzen." Whistler's painting shows a young Western woman wearing Oriental clothes and painting a Chinese vase on her lap. Whistler obviously had no idea at this time how Chinese porcelain was actually manufactured. In any event, Du Maurier's cartoon echoes Whistler's title and recalls the outlandish foreign dress and preoccupation of the young woman in his painting.

Du Maurier's best aesthetic cartoons are those featuring such recurrent characters as Postlethwaite and Maudle. Introduced in 1880, Jellaby Postlethwaite is the aesthetic poet who dedicated his *Latter-Day Sapphics* to the easily flattered and foolish Mrs. Cimabue Brown. His very name suggests his soft, effeminate, lisping character. The cartoon "Nincompoopiana.—The Mutual Admiration Society"[13] captures the shallow essences not only of Postlethwaite (whose deathlike appearance leads Mrs. Brown to see in him a delicate, sad, and poetic soul) but of Maudle (this is the aesthetic painter's first appearance) and Mrs. Brown herself. Our Gallant Colonel, who stands sensibly on the edge of the cartoon, provides the perspective of the outsider, and shares with the reader a point of sympathetic curiosity and exasperation in the face of all the ritualized fawning. In subsequent cartoons Postlethwaite is given to seeing rich symbolism in the lily, an attitude whereby Du Maurier mocks both the Pre-Raphaelite obsession with symbolic flowers in their paintings and poetry and Oscar Wilde's public appearances with a lily or sunflower in his hand. In "An Aesthetic Midday Meal"[14] Postlethwaite is seated at a table in a restaurant, and the caption reads:

At the Luncheon hour, Jellaby Postlethwaite enters a Pastrycook's and calls for a glass of water, into which he puts a freshly-cut lily, and loses himself in contemplation thereof.

| WAITER: | "Shall I bring you anything else, sir?" |
| JELLABY POSTLETHWAITE: | "Thanks, no! I have all I require, and shall soon have done!" |

As in "Nincompoopiana" where Our Gallant Colonel provides the perspective of common sense, this drawing has the other customers and the waiters all stare at Postlethwaite. They are on the side of the artist and his audience who share a common comic victim. In "Postlethwaite's Last Love"[15] the absurd poet tells this related anecdote: "One evening, for want of anything better to say, I told Mrs. Cimabue Brown, in the strictest confidence, that I could sit up all night with a *lily*. She was holding one in her hand, as usual. She was deeply moved. Her eye moistened. She said, 'Quite so!' and wrung my fingers. And it struck her as such a beautiful thought." This is a brilliant little piece of satiric narrative. The sentences grow short, building to the dramatic conclusion of a clichéd response in "Quite so!" With considerable good humor, Du Maurier's cartoons capture the languid poses and trivial ideals of this Wildean poet.

Maudle's subsequent appearance in "Maudle on the Choice of a Profession"[16] shows him to be an older, more fleshly character than he was in "Nincompoopiana." Furthermore, he now dominates the picture as he leans toward Mrs. Brown to impart his aesthetic advice regarding her son: "Why not let him remain for ever content to *exist beautifully*." A true Philistine, Mrs. Brown lionizes the Maudles and the Postlethwaites, but wants her son to have nothing to do with them. Maudle in this cartoon bears a striking resemblance to Oscar Wilde and, like Postlethwaite, who also resembles Wilde, he uses the aesthetic code word "consummately."

One wonders, in this instance, if life does not imitate art. Whistler wondered about the same question, as can be seen in his anecdote: "Mr. Du Maurier and Mr. Wilde happening to meet in the rooms where Mr. Whistler was holding his first exhibition of Venice etchings, the latter brought the two face to face, and taking each by the arm inquired: 'I say, which one of you two invented the other, eh?'"[17] In "The Decay of Lying," published in 1889, Wilde argues that "Art never expresses anything but itself. It has an independent life."[18] Maudle's suggestion that young Mr. Brown should be content to "exist beautifully" is a simple extension of Wilde's aesthetic philosophy: a person himself can be a work of art.

Du Maurier has created several other aesthetic characters to flesh out this group of mutual self-admirers. Peter Pilcox, a sculptor and painter, gave up the profane life of a chemist's assistant to become one of the "rising aesthetes." In "A Reaction in Aesthetics"[19] Pilcox gazes at his latest painting which represents Mrs. Cimabue Brown, bored with lilies, trying to smell a sunflower. "I'm afraid it's one of my failures," Pilcox laments. Mrs. Brown reassures him that "your failures remind one of Michael Angelo at his best!" Pilcox replies, "Not so bad as that, I hope." Since Pilcox and Mrs. Brown are alone in the drawing, with no Gallant Colonel or pictorial public to react to their foolish discussion, Du Maurier simply allows Michaelangelo's reputation to stand as a foil to the pomposity of these two characters.

Mrs. Cimabue Brown appears a total of ten times in *Punch*. Her very name indicates her fragmented and affected personality. Cimabue, of course, is the famous thirteenth-century Florentine painter and mosaicist. Brown, on the other hand, is one of the most common surnames in England. In sum, she is a parody of the taste for Pre-Raphaelite, Italian primitive artists. The most extreme of aesthetic women, Mrs. Brown collects other aesthetes as one might collect paintings. Postlethwaite and Maudle are her two favorites and they respond to her flattery by immortalizing her in their paintings, sculpture, and verse. This peculiar and narcissistic trinity came to depend upon each other for their fictitious existence. Consequently, when Du Maurier finally decided to finish off his aesthetes he did so in a way that touches upon their essential natures. Entitled "Frustrated Social Ambition,"[20] Du Maurier's final aesthetic cartoon in *Punch* depicts Postlethwaite and Maudle clutching each other in grief, a crumpled newspaper in Postlethwaite's hand, and Mrs. Brown, with head bowed, weeping bitterly. The caption reads: "Collapse of Postlethwaite, Maudle, and Mrs. Cimabue Brown, on reading in a widely circulated contemporary journal that they only exist in Mr. Punch's vivid imagination. They had fondly flattered themselves that universal fame was theirs at last."

Another objectionable group of people that Du Maurier took to task were the nouveau riche whose self-interest, unlike that of the aesthetes, was grounded in money, vulgarity, and material ostentation. The characters that Du Maurier created to epitomize this class were Sir Gorgius Midas and Mrs. Ponsonby de Tomkyns. Mrs. Ponsonby de Tomkyns is the modern social spirit, ready to take advan-

tage of everything and everyone that will advance her in society. Her
unfortunate husband is always in the background for he lacks the
imagination and drive of his ingenious wife. In the Darwinian world
of natural selection, Mrs. de Tomkyns is a survivor. Her instincts for
self-preservation are finely tuned and she is as capable of absorbing the
aesthetes as she is of the dukes and duchesses into her ever-growing
circle of influence. The instrument of her successful climb to respectability is the after-dinner entertainment. Employing a variety of
tricks, she manages to engage a series of distinguished musicians and
singers to perform without paying them anything. She convinces
Signor Jenkins to sing at one of her parties by telling him that the
duchess of Stilton, an important patron of the arts, will be in
attendance. On another occasion she uses the performance of a well-
known Italian musician to lure several princesses to her house, and
when her husband protests that he is a "rowdy foreigner" who is
"always pitching into England . . . where he makes all his money,"
she silences him with "No, no! Hush love! He's a genius! He plays the
flageolet better than any man living! The princesses would never have
been here to-night, but for him!—and remember, Ponsonby, he plays
for us for nothing!!!"[21]

Mrs. Ponsonby de Tompkyns's perseverence in applying all of her
social tactics—despite a few failures and despite her lumpish husband—is finally rewarded. The elusive duchess whose presence she is
always courting becomes a good friend and aristocrats and royalty
eventually grace the after-dinner entertainments. The little London
lady realizes her dream and becomes the most sought-after hostess in
the city. Over the years Du Maurier became very fond of his creation.
She held a fascination for him that led him to portray her social
ambitions with a quiet humor that was rounded with genuine respect.
As Henry James noted, "this lady is a real creation. . . . She is
young, very nice-looking, slim, graceful, indefatigable."[22] Her high-
spirited character and intelligence, combined with her beauty, set her
apart from the rest of Du Maurier's satiric characters. She quietly
disappeared from the pages of *Punch*, unlike Maudle, Brown, and
Postlethwaite who made their exit in a fit of mutual despondency.
Kate Greenaway explains that Du Maurier grew "so fond of her in the

end, he could not let the retribution fall upon her that he intended to finish her up with."[23]

Sir Gorgius and Lady Midas, on the other hand, represent the vulgar, tactless, and despised. Whereas Mrs. Ponsonby de Tomkyns was a beautiful, slim woman, the Midases are both fat and ugly. Their touch turns everything that is elegant and splendid into something vulgar and repulsive. Sir Gorgius—his name reflects his rapacious habits of eating and ironically highlights his unpleasant appearance— is a businessman who has apparently made his millions during the reckless industrial growth of earlier decades. This old-time capitalist is blunt and ruthless, but he affects a humility that he believes is expected of his class. In "Humility in Splendour"[24] he and his wife and a minister sit at the Midas dinner table surrounded by six servants and palatial splendor. The centerpiece on the table is an elaborately wrought urn nearly five feet tall and which dominates the illustration. The caption reads: *"The Reverend Lazarus Jones* (who has been honored by an invitation to lunch with that great man, Sir Gorgius Midas, just returned from America). 'I suppose you are glad to get back to your comfortable house again, Sir Gorgius?' *Sir Gorgius Midas* (who perhaps does not like his palatial residence to be called a 'comfortable house') 'Yes, Jones! Be it ever so *'umble*, Jones, there's no place like *'ome!'*"

When the Midas family mixes with the true aristocracy whose manners and language are refined and elegant, the vulgarity of the nouveau riche stands out for ridicule. The aristocracy functions in this series in much the same way that "Our Gallant Colonel" does in the aesthetic cartoons: they both provide the artist's perspective through which the reader understands and laughs at the satiric victim. Having tea with Lady Gwendoline Beaumanoir, Sir Gorgius laments in his lower-class dialect that "society's gettin' much too mixed, yer Lady-ship! I can assure you, when Lady M's a drivin' about London in one of 'er hopen carriages, she 'ardly dares look up, for fear o' seein' someone she knows on the top of a homnibus!" Lady Beaumanoir sharply replies, "Yes, very sad! By the way, I'm afraid she'll often see *Papa* there; but never *me*, you know! Mama and I *always go inside*!"[25]

Du Maurier's favorite device for ridiculing the Midas family is to have Mrs. Ponsonby de Tomkyns snub and outclass them. In "Honour

When Honour Is Due"[26] Mrs. de Tomkyns is lounging securely in a chair as she listens to Sir Gorgius's complaint that he has not been made a Peer: "Why it's enough to make a man turn *radical*, 'anged if it ain't, to think of sich services as mine bein' rewarded with no 'igher title than what's bestowed on a heminent sawbones, or a hingerneer, or a literary man, or even a successful hartist." Mrs. Ponsonby replies sympatheticaly, "It does seem hard! But you've only to bide your time, Sir Gorgius. No man of your stamp need ever despair of a peerage!" On another occasion Du Maurier plays off Mrs. Ponsonby de Tompkyn's superiority in securing after-dinner entertainments. As Sir Gorgius and Lady Midas prepare to leave the party, Lady Midas compliments the star performer: "How charmingly you play, Hare Leebart! Dear Mrs. Ponsonby de Tomkyns must really bring you down to play to us at Midas Towers, our place in Surrey, you know, and—I will show you my roses, the finest roses in all England! Will Thursday suit you?" Herr Leibhardt rejoins: "You are ferry vrently, Matame! Pot I haf a vife and zix jiltren, and—zey to not life upon roses."[27]

Ormond complains that the recurrent jokes at these easy and defenseless targets are at times repellent and reflect a snobbery and social insecurity which demanded a victim.[28] Du Maurier's attacks, however, do not seem any more ruthless or unjustified than those of Dickens and Thackeray upon their socially ambitious and pretentious characters. Du Maurier is a snob and does little to hide the fact. Some of the major characters in his novels (especially Barty Josselin, in *The Martian*) reflect the same sense of superiority. Barty Josselin is Du Maurier's ideal man—handsome, tall, intelligent, witty, sensitive, and, not surprisingly, a proponent of eugenics. Sir Gorgius is a grotesque parody of that ideal, a painful reminder of social and aesthetic imperfection that must be abused, attacked, laughed at. As Henry James noted, Du Maurier "has a peculiar perception of the look of breeding, of race; and that left to himself, as it were, he would ask nothing better than to make it the prerogative of all his characters. For looking out into the world he perceives Sir Gorgius Midas . . . and the whole multitude of the vulgar who have not been cultivated like orchids and race-horses."[29]

There are a large number of foreigners in Du Maurier's cartoons,

mostly comic stereotypes of different national groups. The Frenchman and the German are his two favorites. The Frenchman, of course,
he knows intimately from his own family and from the years he spent
in Paris. Du Maurier's Frenchman is a considerable improvement over
John Leech's Frenchman, whose most outstanding trait was that he
became seasick every time he crossed the Channel. Du Maurier first
distinguishes the physical characteristics of the Frenchman from the
Englishman. The English are usually drawn as lean, tall, angular
figures; whereas the French appear to be short and plump, with short
necks and round stomachs. In "Consequence of the Tower of Babel"[30]
Du Maurier satirizes the Frenchman's notorious trait of refusing
either to learn or to speak English. A young Englishwoman abroad at
a hotel dining room shares this dialogue with a Frenchman sitting next
to her: " 'Parlez-vous Français, mademoiselle?' 'No, Sir.' 'Sprechen
sie Deutsch, Fraulein?' 'No.' 'Habla usted Espagñol, Senorita?' 'No.'
'Parlate Italians, Signorina?' 'No.' Finally she asks him, "Do you
speak English sir?" And he replies, "Helas! Non, Mademoiselle!" and
sighs deeply. In "At Bullong"[31] Du Maurier has another turn at
linguistic play, this time at the expense of the Englishman. Mr.
Belleville, who likes to air his French before his friends, asks a
saleswoman in a French boutique: "Avvyvoo la Parfume du—er—du
Jockey-Club?" The saleslady replies, "O yes, sare! Ve have all ze
English smells!" The Gallic wit is evident again in "British Tourists
Abroad."[32] An Englishman and his wife are in a French shop and the
husband tells his wife to ask the proprietor if he has a directory. In her
broken French she inquires, "Er—esker vous avez le directoire, monsieur?" He answers, "Oh, non, madame. Nous avons la republique, à
present!" Over and over again, the English tourist is rendered as
mute, inexpressive, or awkward in handling the French language or
understanding its culture. The French, consequently, appear superior
and quietly and wittily put the English foreigner in his place. No
matter how high an opinion the English have of themselves, they
usually appear stiff, provincial, and much too serious. Beneath the
humor of these encounters between the two cultures—usually designed as a linguistic duel—Du Maurier seems to side with the highly
civilized Frenchman.

Most of Du Maurier's Germans, on the other hand, are rendered as comic characters, and usually are musicians. Henry James says that he captured "the very temperament of the German pianist,"[33] a figure that appears numerous times at the after-dinner entertainments of Mrs. Ponsonby de Tomkyns and others. Du Maurier, of course, had firsthand experience with visiting foreign musicians when he attended the elegant dinner parties at Tulse Hill and Little Holland House, and in his cartoons he goes to the heart of the temperamental and egotistical nature of the German impressarios. One of his finest pieces is entitled "A Sensitive Plant"[34] depicting Herr Pumpernickel bent over the keyboard of his piano and sobbing dramatically—to the consternation of his English admirers. The caption reads: "(Herr Pumpernickel, having just played a Composition of his own, bursts into Tears.) *Chorus of Friends.* 'Oh, what is the matter? What can we do for you?' *Herr Pumpernickel.* 'Ach! Nossing! Nossing! Bot ven I hear really *coot* music, zen must I always veep!'" As in his French cartoons Du Maurier enjoys the misunderstandings that come about in the clash of two languages. In "At Loss for a Word"[35] the satire stings both the German musician and the English lady who just completed a performance at the piano: "*Distinguished Foreigner.* 'Ach! Meess! I goncratulate you vrom de pottom of my harrt!!! You have blayed and zung kvite—kvite—' *Fair Performer.* 'Quite execrably?' *Distinguished Foreigner.* 'Ach! Yes! Dafs is de vortp—quite exekraply'" Most of Du Maurier's Germans resemble each other: they are short and stocky with full faces and heavy mustaches. Many of them look like Albert Einstein, with his round, dark eyes and slightly drooping, heavy eyelids, and bushy eyebrows. When he came to write *Trilby* Du Maurier resurrected the character of the comic German in the person of Herr Kreutzer, supposedly a well-known composer, who sings the praises of Trilby: "*All* music is koot ven *she* zings it."[36] Du Maurier's most famous foreign character is Svengali, a Polish Jew, but this complex figure will be examined later.

Almost as foreign to Du Maurier as the French and Germans are the English clergy. Although he was raised in a Christian household, the skepticism which Du Maurier felt as a young man finally blossomed into an aggressive agnosticism by the 1890s. His loss of any religious faith and acceptance of Darwinism led him to devote many didactic pages of his novels, especially in *The Martian*, to an attack upon traditional Christianity. His drawings in *Punch*, however, reflect a much lighter tone and mood, and suggest that Du Maurier's attitude in the 1870s and 1880s was more tolerant of the clergy at that time. A typical figure is the shy curate who, in one cartoon, comes to a house on parish business and is told by Miss Margaret that "I'm *so* sorry Mama and my sisters are out!" He then proceeds to put his foot in his mouth by remarking, "Oh, pray don't mention it. *One* of the family is *quite* enough!"[37] On another occasion the young curate is addressed by his older clergyman host: "I'm afraid you've got a bad egg, Mr. Jones." Exercising his true humility, the curate replies, "Oh no, my lord, I assure you! Parts of it are excellent!"[38] Du Maurier's curates are usually on the defensive. Shy and unassuming, they are saddled with all the menial tasks of the parish, and Du Maurier sympathizes with their tentative position in society and treats them with a gentle humor.

The bishop, on the other hand, comes in for a more telling blow. Visiting the home of a somewhat carelessly outspoken old woman, he is told: "Ah, Bishop, what a heavenly sermon that was of yours last Sunday, about worldliness and the vanities of flesh!—it nearly made me cry! And I say, Bishop, *how hard it hit you and me*!!!"[39] The influence of the bishop comes under attack in "Effect of Episcopal Influence."[40] In a busy street scene, the bishop is pictured riding through the crowds from which he claims another member for his church: "It's all very well to become a radical or an atheist, and all that; but a Bishop's a Bishop! So at least poor Todeson finds out, when the Bishop of Clapham . . . takes him for someone else, and favours him with a gracious wave of the hand—thereby reclaiming him to the bosom of the established Church." The bishop appears in several other cartoons and Du Maurier rounds his personality by showing him dealing with the worldly affairs of his family. Like Lord Chesterfield, he gives his youngest and favorite son some practical advice about the choice of a profession: "Now, why shouldn't you adopt the stage as a profession, Theodore? Lord Ronald Beaumanoir, who's a year younger than yourself, is already getting sixteen guineas a week for low comedy parts at the Criterion! The Duchess told me so herself only yesterday!" The cartoon is appropriately entitled "Tempora Mutantor."[41] The fact that the times are changing is brought home to the

bishop himself in a later cartoon in which he attempts to lecture the
son of an American lady aboard ship in mid-Atlantic: "When I was
your age, my young friend, it was not considered good manners for
little boys to join in the conversation of grown-up people, unless they
were invited to do so. The small American boy looks up at the bishop
and says, "Guess that was seventy or eighty years ago. We've changed
all that, you bet."[42] In a later cartoon entitled "Our Curates,"[43] Du
Maurier allows this oppressed group to deliver the final, if ephemeral,
blow to the vicars and bishops who run the church. Standing with legs
apart in a posture of great strength and determination, a curate
addresses a seated acquaintance: "My Vicar's away! I preach three
times on Sunday, and boss the entire show."

Given Du Maurier's conservatism, it comes as no surprise that the
liberated woman and the subject of women's rights come in for
ridicule. Curates and bishops may be guilty of an occasional breach of
good manners, but for women to demand an equal social footing with
men was a cardinal sin against the status quo that gave the solidity to
Du Maurier's world. In "Taking Time by the Forelock"[44] Du Maurier
expresses his hostility toward women in the professions. A young girl
reports to her mother that "Uncle George says every woman ought to
have a profession, and I think he's quite right." Her bravado is
diminished, however, when she explains, "I mean to be a professional
beauty." Beauty, domesticity, and a loving character were the attributes in women prized by Du Maurier. In another cartoon the attractive Cousin Bella admires the opinion of Mr. Fibson who told her he
could not bear intellectual women: "He said woman's mission was to
be beautiful."[45] In "The Coming Race"[46] Du Maurier depicts the
reversal of the sexes in the profession of medicine. The drawing
suggests one relationship between the man and woman but the
caption undercuts that initial suggestion. In the illustration one sees a
young lady dressed in all her Victorian finery—from bustle to hat
trimmed with roses—looking in a beseeching manner up at a tall,
dominant man dressed in a practical business suit. The caption
reads: "*Dr. Evangeline.* 'By the bye, Mr. Sawyer, are you engaged
to-morrow afternoon? I have rather a ticklish operation to perform—
an amputation, you know.' *Mr. Sawyer.* 'I shall be very happy to do it
for you.' *Dr. Evangeline.* 'O, no, not *that*! But will you kindly come

and administer the chloroform for me?' " Du Maurier gets away with a neat visual trick, one that works even today when women physicians are more common.

The intellectual woman is cleverly ridiculed in "The Higher Education of Women"[47] where Jones asks Miss Jessica if she saw the star-showers the other night. Miss Jessica makes a rapid but comprehensive survey of the heavens and replies, "No, but it couldn't have been much, for there are no stars missing." In "Terrible Result of the Higher Education of Women"[48] Du Maurier shows a group of beautiful women being escorted by older men past a line of frustrated handsome young men. Miss Hypatia Jones, "Spinster of Arts," informs her companion, Professor Parallax, that "young men do very well to look at, or to dance with, or even to marry, and all that kind of thing! But as to enjoying any rational conversation with any man under fifty, *that* is *completely* out of the question!"

All of the women in the cartoons described above are beautiful and graceful, but their commitment to intellectual pursuits is made to seem both incongruous and superficial. When Du Maurier draws a feminist leader, however, his pencil becomes more cruel. Miss Gander Bellweather, "the famous champion of women's rights, the future founder of a new philosophy," is an extremely ugly, masculine-looking figure. She gathers around her the young intellectuals of the day, all of whom are ugly and weak-looking little men. Standing at the edge of the drawing, a handsome young lady remarks to Captain Dandelion: "Isn't it a pretty sight to see the rising young geniuses of the day all flocking to her side, and hanging on her lips, and feasting on the sad and earnest utterances wrung from her indignant heart by the wrongs of her wretched sex?" Captain Dandelion finds the whole affair distasteful and remarks: "Wather pwefer *she*-women myself—wather pwefer the wretched sex with all its wongs—haw!"[49]

If, in Du Maurier's drawings, the advocates of women's rights look like ugly men, the beautiful women who follow the feminist line and assert their equal rights are made to look foolish by appearing to parody men. "The Fair Sex-Tett,"[50] for example, shows "the accomplishments of the rising Female Generation." Six elegantly dressed and coiffured young ladies are depicted giving a musical performance before an exclusively male audience. Although most of the men are listening attentively, one man is seen leaning out of his box watching the six beauties through a pair of binoculars. This is one of several cartoons that trivializes the accomplishments of the women's movement. Another drawing is based upon the sacred Victorian institution of the men's club. Du Maurier presents a female club—another imagined accomplishment of women's push for equal rights—in which Miss Firebrace, reclining in a lounge chair, addresses her friend, Julia: "Send your horse home, and stop and dine with me, Julia! I've asked Trixy Rattlecash and Emily Sheppard." Julia, with a sigh of regret for the freedom of spinsterhood and the charms of club life, replies, "Can't, my dear girl! My sainted old father-in-law's just gone back to Yorkshire, and poor Bolly's all alone!"[51] Silly and ridiculous as all of these cartoon women are, Du Maurier obviously saw the feminist movement as a threat to the established order of Victorian society. His ideal of womanhood, on the other hand, is one that will be discussed later as part of his private world. His beautiful woman dominates both his drawings and his novels. The political woman is one he did not know well and her demands were never clearly understood by Du Maurier. Consequently, the fiery flesh-and-blood reality of actual feminists he tamed and transformed through caricature.

Du Maurier rarely draws the lower classes. Not only did his editor advise him not to, but Du Maurier himself did not know or even care to know that group. He found them to be ugly, dirty, noisy, and threatening. And that is how they are portrayed in the few cartoons he did of them. But Du Maurier did know the lower classes as represented by the servants, who were a vital part of the upper-class world. He and others on the *Punch* staff set forth the comedy of upstairs versus downstairs that exhibited the misunderstandings and feelings that existed between servant and master. Although frequently patronizing in his tone, Du Maurier nevertheless sympathized with the outspoken and sometimes exploited group so necessary in the maintenance of genteel households. The servants of Sir Gorgius Midas suffer rather outrageous treatment, as befits his brutal attitude toward those less fortunate than he. Coming home at two in the morning, he is outraged to find only four footmen to greet him at the door: "A pretty state of things, indeed!" he exclaims to the head footman. "So that if I'd a' 'appened to brought 'ome a friend, there'd a' only been you four to led us hin, hay!"[52] Under the guise of sentimentality, the footman is made to suffer again, this time at the hands of a tender-hearted and impulsive lady who orders him to behave like an animal: "You see this poor kitten the children have found? It is motherless! Get some milk, Thomas! Mew like its mother—and feed it!"[53] The cartoon is, of course, satirical but it also reveals the patronizing attitudes of the upper-class toward their servants. Despite the humor, there is an unpleasant tone to the cartoon that seems to reflect Du Maurier's own sense of superiority. Sometimes it is the improper use of language by a servant that delights the author, as in this dialogue between a lady and a prospective servant: " 'Yes, mum, father kept an inn at Little Peddington, and mother kept the post-office there.' 'And your late master—who and what was he?' 'The Reverend Mr. Wilkins, Ma'am. He kept a vicarage at Medlingham, close by!' " The cartoon is ironically entitled "A New Trade."[54]

When Du Maurier allows his servants a sweet moment of revenge upon their masters, he chooses the Midas family for his victim. In "A Butler's Revenge"[55] the butler brings a tray to Lady Midas who is seated right next to an important visitor: " 'Well, Rivers, what are these?' *Rivers (who has received warning).* 'The decanter stoppers, my Lady. Just after the gentlemen left the dining-room to jine the ladies, Sir Gorgius locked up the decanters, as usual, but he forgot the stoppers; so I thought I'd better bring 'em up to your Ladyship!' " When the servant class is depicted talking among themselves they sometimes exhibit their own version of snobbery. In "Self-Respect"[56] a cook asks a fellow servant who has just returned from an interview for a new position if she is going to accept the job: "Not if I knows it! Why, when I got there, blest if there wasn't the two young ladies of the 'ouse both a' usin' of one piano at the same time: 'Well,' thinks I, 'this *his* a comin' down in the world.' So I thought I was best say good mornin'!" Most of Du Maurier's servants, except for a few of the young women, are drawn with a great deal of individual character. Unlike the majority of his upper-class figures who resemble each other, the servants have strikingly different features, sizes, shapes, and clothing. The beautiful upper classes, on the other hand, have lost some of their individuality because they are drawn according to Du Maurier's fixed ideal of the aristocracy.

Du Maurier's public world—the society pictures surveyed above—served as the basis for much that appears in his three novels. The character of Joe Sibley in *Trilby*, for example, while based upon James Whistler, owes a great deal to Du Maurier's satire of the aesthetic movement. A bohemian nonconformist, Sibley is described as "the idle apprentice,"[57] beauty being an end in itself. Du Maurier's drawing of Sibley also captures the qualites of his aesthetic cartoons, with their emphasis upon outlandish dress and affected postures. The nouveau riche also reappear in his novel, though there are no characters as crude and vulgar as Sir Gorgius Midas. But the narrator of *The Martian*, Sir Robert Maurice, announces "I'm a Philistine and not ashamed."[58] Du Maurier nevertheless treats this character with the same respect and gentle satire that he reserved for Mrs. Ponsonby de Tomkyns. There are a few comic foreigners in the novels, like Herr Kreutzer, but Du Maurier's most famous foreigner, Svengali, is a serious, menacing figure. When Du Maurier attempts to treat him humorously, the humor quickly degenerates to a cruel and savage satire that fails to disguise the author's loathing of this Polish Jew. The gentle satire of the clergymen in *Punch* also degenerates into an extended serious attack upon Christianity in the novels. In *Trilby*, for instance, Little Billee proclaims his agnosticism in the presence of a country vicar who finally exclaims, "You're trying to *rob me of my Saviour*! Never you dare to darken *my* door-step again!"[59]

The subject of women's rights, on the other hand, does not arise in the novels. Du Maurier essentially relinquished the role of satirist when he began writing, and the women he depicts in his novels are all very serious, beautiful, and idealized characters. They are a vital part of his dream world—as will be shown later—and consequently, he shuts out the threatening feminist from his idealized world. The servants and lower classes also do not play a prominent part in his novels. Trilby, of course, is a major exception. She is a servant girl who is magically transformed into a magnificent singer and thus wins the adulation of the upper and aristocratic classes. In his society pictures Du Maurier attempted to portray everyone from the aesthetes to the servants as comic stereotypes and, with a clever caption, he satirized them. His novels, on the other hand, are more concerned with ideals and dreams, reflections of his inner nature that he only rarely exhibited in his drawings.

Dream Pictures

Du Maurier depicted two sorts of dream visions in his cartoons for *Punch*: the idealized family and the private terrors of the nightmare.

The former drawings were mostly based upon his own family life while he resided in Hampstead. The cartoons with the grotesque figures, on the other hand, seem to represent Du Maurier's childlike anxieties and fears. Both sets of drawings provide a direct link to the major themes of his novels: the search for a lost, dreamlike innocence of youth, and the powerful influence of the unconscious upon one's thoughts and behavior.

The powerful nostalgia that dominates his novels first surfaced in the Hampstead drawings Du Maurier did for *Punch* beginning in the 1870s. "Hampstead was my Passy," he wrote, "the Leg-of-Mutton Pond my Mare d'Auteuil."[60] Du Maurier hoped that Hampstead would recreate for his children the same rustic charm he enjoyed as a child in Passy. The quiet woods, the magical lake where he day-dreamed for hours, the bumblebees and bright flowers, the overriding sense of peace and harmony, and the sure knowledge that his mother was there in the background to take care of him—this idyllic atmosphere now belonged to his own family and he memorialized it in numerous drawings. The past, it seemed, could be recaptured after all and the dream made a reality.

The Hampstead drawings faithfully reproduce the elegant lawns and landscape of the region. It is a very civilized nature that we see there, with occasional long, dramatic shadows cast by the trees or by the children in the evenings that suggest a vague and mysterious brooding. Most of the scenes present Du Maurier's wife and children and the captions record some of their actual dialogue. It is noteworthy that Du Maurier himself is absent from most of these drawings. In Passy the scenes were the same: the Du Maurier children playing under the watchful eyes of their mother, the father usually away. The dominant role of his mother thus reasserts itself in the pictures of his wife, Emma, the beautiful, reassuring center of domestic gravity in Hampstead. These cartoons are not satirical or critical like those which focus on the public world. Rather, they are studies of child-hood simplicity and innocence. Some of the captions are humorous and reflect the child's unaffected and sometimes embarrassingly di-rect manner of speaking his or her mind. High-spirited and occasion-ally tough-minded, the Du Maurier children do not resemble the sentimentalized children that dominated so many Victorian bad paintings. Du Maurier's domestic cartoons present a family that is not only very attractive, but one that is intelligent, sensitive, and articulate.

In a cartoon entitled "Egoism,"[61] a small girl asserts her independence in no uncertain terms. Her brother calls, "Come here, Dora! I wants you!" And Dora replies, "Thank you, Eric; but I wants myself!" Attractively drawn, little Dora comes across as a real child, well-mannered but an individual with her own way of thinking. "A Whispered Appeal,"[62] one of the best-drawn cartoons of the 1870s, depicts a young girl pleading with her mother not to punish her little brother who has been made to stand in the corner: "Mamma! Mamma! *Don't* scold him any more! It makes the room so dark!" The caption brilliantly reflects the child's anxiety. The perspective of the drawing—with its low eye level from which the reader looks up at the dominant figure of the mother bending to hear her daughter's quiet appeal—reinforces the child's point of view.

When Du Maurier shifts the scenes out of doors the drawings become more vibrant. In "Delicate Consideration"[63] he depicts his five children in a line playing train. Beatrix, the oldest child, is the engine and she explains to her mother what they are doing: "O Mamma, we're playing at railway trains. I'm the engine and Guy's a first-class carriage, and Sylvia's a second-class carriage, and May's a third-class carriage, and Gerald, he's a third-class carriage, too—that is, he's really only a *truck*, you know, only you mustn't tell him so, as it would offend him." Perhaps dressed up somewhat, Beatrix's explanation nevertheless reveals the same keen awareness of social levels that her father possesses. But the picture itself carries more of a tale than does the caption, for it presents a sunny, pastoral atmosphere conducive to high-spirited play. The dominant figure of the idealized Emma stands at the right edge of the drawing, thus carrying the line of figures across the page from the smallest to the tallest. As in Passy, it never rains in the idealized Hampstead countryside. One cartoon shows a little boy standing in a field adjoining the house. His tall, beautiful mother tells him that it threatens to rain and that they had better go indoors. But the boy asserts that it won't rain because "Papa always threatens to vip me! But he never does."[64]

In reading the opening chapters of *Peter Ibbetson* where Du Maurier recounts his childhood in Passy, one recalls these Hampstead children and their beautiful mother, set against the quiet, dreamlike landscape: figures that exist in the artist's memories of his own childhood as much as they do on the smooth slopes of Hampstead itself. They are, in a sense, his dream figures, not unlike the ones that Peter Ibbetson visits in Passy. But dreams are supple, elusive creations and it only requires a slight shift of light and line to render them nightmares. Even some of the idyllic Hampstead scenes contain the dark edges and ominous hints of the grotesque, shadowy world of nightmare. "A Cousinly Hint,"[65] for example, shows a young boy and girl out walking at evening through a grove of tall trees. Their backlighted figures cast shadows along with those of the trees. There is a house visible behind the trees but it is totally black. There is a touch of gothic eeriness about the scene in its dramatic contrasts of light and shadow and in its solitude. Even though the caption is intended as humorous—the girl says that their shadows are "tall enough for us to be married, I think"—it suggests the end of childhood. The two figures face a dark and ominous future as they follow their shadows into the grove—and into adulthood.

The true nightmare drawings are few in number. The most horrifying one is ironically entitled "A Little Christmas Dream."[66] It shows a six-year-old boy's terrifying vision of a two-headed prehistoric monster slowly pursuing him in the snow. Huge clumps of snow build up around the boy's feet so that he cannot outrun the enormous predator. A man in a top hat twirling his cane casually strolls past the monster. The drawing captures the classic anxiety dream of inescapable horror. The end of the trunk of the pre-Adamic hairy elephant is a vicious dragonlike head with its mouth open as if about to swallow the boy. An elephant's trunk is a curious and grotesque item in itself—the natural function of which might be baffling to a young child, but in the dream its deadly purpose is terrifyingly clear as it is about to eat the child. All of the houses in the background are darkened. People are asleep—except for the nonchalant nightwalker—and the moon lights up the snow and reflects on the brow and tusks of the beast. There are a few barren trees visible against the dark sky. The bright, peaceful vision of Passy has been displaced, and there is no comforting mother to make things right in this menacing picture.

Du Maurier also drew a series of four cartoons in *Punch* dealing with the adventures of a Mr. Jenkins, who is flung from his cab when his horse collapses and who subsequently has several nightmares.[67] One drawing conveys the maddening sense of ambiguity so often experienced in dreams. Jenkins has a vision of a colossal and horrifying cab-horse moving down a narrow London alley, and he cannot be sure if he is riding in the cab or standing, powerless to move, directly in front of the raging creature. The next dream shows the horse spinning violently around in a circle, totally out of control, but in the subsequent dream Jenkins is about to kill the animal, which has exhausted itself and has become an easy prey. The Jenkins cartoons, like "A Little Christmas Dream," are violent and exhibit one's anxiety about the natural order of things. Unthinking, powerful creatures are unleashed upon a boy and a man. The horse—man's servant—turns upon its master with deadly rage. One might speculate that the Jenkins cartoons reveal Du Maurier's fear of the lower classes. Once out of control, they pose a danger to the stability of the upper classes and therefore must be kept in harness. On a psychological level, these cartoons may reveal a sexual anxiety as the powerful emotions run rampant and threaten to overwhelm him. Finally the emotions are exhausted and the beast destroyed. What these drawings reveal about Du Maurier, however, cannot be known with any certainty; but their visual impact is considerable and demonstrate the artist's interest in the unconscious mind.

Du Maurier drew one other nightmare scene about this time, "Old Nick-Otin Stealing 'Away the Brains' of His Devotees" (1869).[68] In a darkened room several men are engaged in a smoking orgy. Their pipes have turned into long snakes that go from their mouths to wind about their bodies. The top of each man's head is on fire and one person's head has been completely burned out. He sits slumped in a chair, his empty, bowllike head sending up a final plume of smoke. In the background stands a blackened figure playing a fiery violin. His bow is a thin, clay pipe. Self-indulgence leads to self-consumption in a horribly graphic manner here. Once again, the terror of the scene derives from the collapse of reason and control, as civilized behavior gives way to self-inflicted violence.

Du Maurier's fascination with dreams and nightmares extended into his novels. The central theme in *Peter Ibbetson* is the power of the dreaming mind to capture the past and make it a present reality. Peter spends his life mastering the art of "dreaming true." There is also a powerful nightmare scene in the novel where two hideous dwarfs attempt to kill Peter. Du Maurier effects the same sense of inescapable horror in that passage as he does in his *Punch* cartoons. Nightmares are also of central importance in *Trilby* where the heroine is tormented by evil dreams of Svengali, who appears to her as an incubus and as a black spider with a human head. And in Du Maurier's last novel, *The Martian*, Barty Josselin communicates with a being from another planet through his dreams. The unconscious, as it reveals itself through dreams, nightmares, or—thanks to Svengali—under hypnosis, was one of Du Maurier's abiding interests, and his explorations of the subject provide significant insights into the newly developing psychological literature.

There is one recurrent figure in Du Maurier's drawings that appears in both his social satires and domestic scenes—and later, in all of his novels—and that is the figure of the beautiful woman. Du Maurier's own mother was very attractive and he idealized her in his drawings by making her taller and more graceful looking than she already was. Later he did the same thing for his wife Emma. Beautiful in real life, Emma became a perfect figure in *Punch*: tall, aristocratic, serene, fastidiously dressed, gentle, and loving. Du Maurier acknowledged that "of all my little piebald puppets the one I value most is my pretty woman."[69]

Besides the obvious models of his mother and wife, Du Maurier had a third model which, when combined with the others, caught the essence of his perfect lady. He kept on the mantelpiece of his studio at home a three-foot tall replica of the Venus of Milo: "She is but lightly clad, and what simple garment she wears is not in the fashion of our day. How well I know her! Almost thoroughly by this time—for she has been the silent companion of my work for thirty years."[70] It is the paradigm of her classical beauty and "incarnate virtue" that guides his pen in drawing the thousands of individual beautiful women in *Punch* and other magazines. His Beatrix, for *Henry Esmond*, his transformed

Trilby, his duchess of Towers and Martia, his mother and Emma all share the aristocratic and formal beauty of this ancient sculptured goddess. Du Maurier's ideal woman, however, is rendered in meticulous details that reflect the Victorian age: hair-styles, bustles, floral dresses, elegant lace evening gowns, and long gloves. But beneath these temporal accidents, so to speak, lies the archetypal beauty of the secular saint that transcends the period.

A true romantic, Du Maurier explains his frustration in attempting to render the ideal woman within the limits of his craft:

Like all the best of its kind, and its kind the best, she never sates nor palls, and the more I look at her the more I see to love and worship—and, also, the more dissatisfied I feel—not indeed with the living beauty, ripe and real, that I see about and around—mere life is such a beauty in itself that no stone ideal can ever hope to match it! But dissatisfied with the means at my command to do the living beauty justice—a little bit of paper, a steel pen, and a bottle of ink—and, alas, fingers and an eye less skilled than they would have been if I had gone straight to a school of art instead of a laboratory for chemistry![71]

Henry James was fascinated by Du Maurier's graceful women. He notes that "they all look alike, that they are always sisters—all products of a single birth." Perhaps unaware of Du Maurier's debt to Venus of Milo, James nevertheless intuited the classical ancestor of the beautiful women when he remarked that they "have an inestimable look of repose, a kind of Greek serenity." He observes of a youthful aunt in a *Punch* cartoon: "Her charming pose, the way her head slowly turns, the beautiful folds of her robe, make her look more like a statuette in a museum than like a figure in *Punch*."[72]

Inveterate and imperturbably graceful, Du Maurier's women remain the emotional and aesthetic centers of both his drawings and his novels. His beautiful woman is an idealized composite of mother, lover, and saint. She is devoid of sexuality and does not appear to be made of flesh and blood. Only in his pictures of the servants and lower classes does he depict individuals: pot-bellies, fat faces, gaunt faces, wrinkled clothes abound, and the reader is reminded of the actual world. Du Maurier's great reverence for women and the upper classes, however, leads him to move away from the actual to the ideal. Like many of his Victorian counterparts—Coventry Patmore, Rossetti, and Morris—Du Maurier had elevated the woman to the level of secular saint, whose beauty was to be adored and whose mind was to be ignored.

The Duchess of Towers, *Peter Ibbetson*

Chapter Three
Peter Ibbetson

The Birth of a Novelist

Du Maurier's friends as well as the public were surprised when the famous *Punch* artist suddenly, at age fifty-five, wrote his first novel. Its appearance in *Harper's Monthly* in 1891 led his friend and neighbor Kate Greenaway to say, "I have always liked Mr. Du Maurier, but to think there was all *this*, and one didn't know it. I feel as if I had all this time been doing him a great injustice—not to know."[1] Henry James, whose friendship with Du Maurier during the eighties may well have influenced him to take up the novel, expressed his pleasant surprise as follows: "It is not more easy to start at fifty-five than at twenty-five, and the grammar of any liberal art is not a study to be postponed. Difficult is it, in a word, at any time of life to master a mutinous form and express an uncommon meaning." "The case therefore," James concludes, "demands some attention when people begin to dash off brilliant novels in the afternoon of existence."[2]

There are probably several reasons why Du Maurier began the new career as novelist at this late date. For one thing there was his recurrent anxiety over his eyesight, and he was experiencing some difficulty in coming up with the two weekly cartoons for *Punch*. Money was another factor. For most of his life Du Maurier felt financially insecure, a sense probably rooted in his childhood and his father's improvidence. A successful novel offered him the opportunity to provide a comfortable income for his family in their later years which, like the dark, were quickly approaching.

Still, it would be a mistake to attribute his writing simply to practical concerns. For a quarter of a century he had been shaping in the pages of *Punch*, an image of fashionable society, made up of an array of characters and relationships, which had the power of a captioned slide show, a series of literary still lifes. The novel allowed him to bring continuity, movement, and extended dialogue into his pictures. Most important of all, the novel gave him the opportunity to explore the mind and the potential of its unconscious forces. He was fascinated by the mystery of dreams all his life and only occasionally, as in his cartoon, "A Little Christmas Dream" in *Punch* in 1868, did he express this interest in his drawings. His role on the magazine as satirist of fashionable society did not encourage nor was the magazine the appropriate medium for his investigation of mental phenomena. A romantic by nature, Du Maurier saw the connection between dreams and his lost youth, and the further he got from his childhood the more intense, it seems, was his need to re-create it with all his faculties, and this now extended to the written word.

When he was twenty-seven years old Du Maurier published his first and only piece of fiction in *Once A Week*. "Recollections of An English Goldmine" is an amusing short story based upon the author's experiences at the North Molton Gold Mine, where he worked briefly as an assayer. His friends and associates praised the story and he became convinced that his future lay in writing stories which he would illustrate. The next year he wrote and illustrated a short story about his art student days in Paris with Tom Lamont and Tom Armstrong. Encouraged by Charles Keene, he sent the manuscript to the *Cornhill Magazine*, then edited by William Makepeace Thackeray. The story was rejected and *Once A week* later turned it down also. Du Maurier apparently was crushed by the double rejection, for not only has the manuscript disappeared but he was not to write another story for thirty years. One could only speculate what sort of writer Du Maurier would have become had Thackeray accepted the story and encouraged him. He would have likely become a more polished craftsman. On the other hand, the thirty-year delay probably contributed to the richness of his characters and settings.

As was explained earlier, the immediate stimulus for writing *Peter Ibbetson* came from Henry James. After being urged by the famous American to attempt writing a novel, Du Maurier turned to his memories of his childhood in the Paris suburbs of Passy. The sounds, smells, colors, and texture of those golden days were all carefully recorded. The next morning, however, when he reread what he had written without apparent conscious effort he became skeptical of its value and wandered through his garden at Hampstead wondering whether the work was worth continuing. He then saw a small wheelbarrow, which he took for a good omen because he had described a toy wheelbarrow in his first chapter. Peter Ibbetson, age seven, is depicted on the title page pushing this wheelbarrow and it is described in the novel as if it contained the essence of the author's childhood: "For in the old shed full of tools and lumber at the end of the garden, and half-way between an empty fowl-house and a disused table (each an Eden in itself) I found a small toy-wheelbarrow—quite the most extraordinary, the most unheard of and undreamed of, humorously, daintily, exquisitely fascinating object I had ever come across in all my brief existence."[3] Du Maurier would have delighted in William Carlos Williams's lines, "So much depends / upon a red wheelbarrow. . . ."

The first draft of *Peter Ibbetson* was completed during the summer of 1889. Du Maurier wrote quickly giving little time for revision. He read his work to several friends, Canon Alfred Ainger, Basil Champneys, and Henry James, and they all advised him to publish the novel. He sent the manuscript to Harper's in April, 1890, and the publishers forwarded it to their literary agent, James Ripley Osgood, with Du Maurier's covering letter:

> I have no notion whether it is suited to a periodical or not—you will see; probably *not*,—but if it is I want to be well paid for it. . . . If *Harper's* doesn't see its way to it, I shall offer it elsewhere; and after that, I shall put it in the hands of an agent. And if I don't get what I think I ought to, I shall keep it and write another, as I have several good ideas, and writing this has taught me a lot. All of which sounds very cheeky and grand; but I am in no hurry to come before the public as a novelist before I'm ripe, and to ripen myself duly I am actually rewriting it in French, and you've no idea what a lesson *that* is![4]

Du Maurier's tough stance was unnecessary because Osgood liked the novel, and asked the author to supply his own illustrations. It appeared in *Harper's Monthly* from June to December of 1891, and was published in a two-volume book edition without illustrations the same year. A cheaper one-volume edition with illustrations appeared in October, 1891, published by Harper's subsidiary, Osgood McIlvaine.

Du Maurier's close friends wrote notes of congratulations upon his formal entry into the world of published authors. He also received letters from many readers, especially from Americans, expressing their pleasure with the work. The intriguing idea of a dream life appealed greatly to all his new admirers, but there were many who criticized what they referred to as the supernatural part of the book. Still, the initial sales of the novel were not exceptional. It was only after the wild success of *Trilby* that the first novel became popular.

The Theme of Duality

The story of *Peter Ibbetson* is told from the point of view of Gogo Pasquier, later given the English name of Peter Ibbetson, who is a convicted murderer writing his memoirs in his prison cell. The work is introduced by his fictional cousin-editor, Madge Plunket. The novel opens with a description of the idyllic Passy where Gogo spends the first seven years of his life. The only child of an English mother and French father, Gogo spends much of his time in the company of his neighbor, the beautiful Madame Seraskier and her ungainly daughter Mimsey. These pastoral days come to an abrupt end when his father is killed by the explosion of a safety lamp of his own invention and the subsequent death of his mother, who dies while being delivered of a still-born child, a week later. Madame Seraskier, meanwhile, dies of cholera and Mimsey goes to Russia with her father.

Colonel Ibbetson, a relative of Gogo's mother, arranges to educate and make a gentleman of Gogo in England and begins by having the boy assume the name Peter Ibbetson. After completing his studies Peter works as an apprentice architect for a Mr. Lintot in the dreary town of Pentonville. He finds both his work and environment so depressing he begins to establish a secret inner life based upon art, music, and memories of Passy. His friendships, romance, and ambition all come to naught in Pentonville, until one day he visits the fashionable estate of Lady Cray to make some architectural plans. During this first glimpse of society he sees the most beautiful woman of his life, the duchess of Towers.

Peter returns to Passy in an attempt to revisit the past but discovers that both the people and the place have changed for the worse. The old apple tree in the garden under whose boughs he and Mimsey spent delightful hours playing and reading is now a mere stump. That night in his hotel room Peter dreams of the duchess of Towers, who explains to him how he can "dream true," that is, return to the past, experience it, and see himself there, provided he does not touch or alter anything. And in this dream he returns to the garden of Passy and sees his parents, himself, Madame Seraskier, and Mimsey, though they, of course, do not see him.

Back in London, he meets the duchess of Towers again at Lady Cray's, only this time they talk to each other and discover each other's identity. She is, of course, Mimsey Seraskier, as tall and beautiful as her mother, and the woman who haunts Peter's dreams. Although they seldom meet in the world, Peter and she henceforth meet at almost every sleeping moment of their lives, two people who share one world in their mutual dreams.

At this point in the novel, the external life of the hero is summarily dealt with, and the focus shifts to Peter's dreams, his mental life which he so perfectly shares with the duchess. Still, there are some important external details that need to be disclosed. Peter reads an old letter from Colonel Ibbetson that implies that Peter is his illegitimate son. Peter confronts the colonel with the letter, they fall into a violent argument, and Peter kills him in self-defense. He is condemned to die but the sentence is commuted to life imprisonment. The details of his twenty-five years in prison are given scant attention, for his imaginative life takes command. He lives now only to sleep, to dream, to spend fantastic hours with the duchess of Towers. They not only revisit this past but adventure further down time to visit the world of their grandparents in France. They spend time with great authors, artists, and musicians of the past, and even have their own dream-home, Magna sed Apta, a palace of art decked out with historical treasures.

Finally this dream world is crushed, even as that of Passy was years earlier, when the duchess of Towers dies. No longer able to "dream true," Peter is on the verge of suicide when she returns from death to enliven his hope. During this final encounter, this last dream, she explains to him the superiority of the bodiless form, of life unlimited by time and space. Their true joy and unity is yet to come. Peter dies happy and fulfilled: "A cell in a criminal lunatic asylum! That does not sound like a bower in the Elysian Fields! It is, and has been for me" (416).

The first half of the novel is factual, full of precise descriptions and details that often appear to have little connection with the central plot. It is almost totally autobiographical as Du Maurier lovingly reconstructs his childhood in Passy and contrasts those years with his unhappy days in Pentonville when, from age seventeen to twenty-two, he tried to master a technical vocation. The illusion of reality in these early scenes is so powerful that it survives the sudden melodramatic shift when Peter murders Colonel Ibbetson, goes to prison for life, and learns the secret of "dreaming true." The second half of the novel matter-of-factly introduces and develops the subject of astonishing psychic phenomena.

The two-part structure of the novel is significant because it both supports and reflects the central theme of the work: the split personality. First of all there is a cultural duality in Peter's parentage: "My tall and beautiful young mother . . . was an Englishwoman who had been born and partly brought up in Paris. My gay and jovial father . . . was a Frenchman, although an English subject, who had been born and partly brought up in London" (25). Peter embodies this duality within himself. He is bilingual and his memoirs are rich with French dialogue and descriptions. Interestingly, his only attempt to unify the two languages comes in his childhood relationship with Mimsey—but even here the duality persists: " . . . Mimsey, who was full of resource, invented a new language, or rather two, which we call Frankingle and Inglefrank, respectively. They consisted in anglicizing French nouns and verbs and then conjugating and pronouncing them Englishly, or *vice versa*" (40).

Peter also embodies the two cultures of his parents. His emotional life is centered in France, in Passy. The memorable pond "La Mare d'Auteuil," Louis Philippe's Bois de Boulogne, and the "magical combination of river, bridge, palace, gardens, mountain, and forest,

St. Cloud" are fixed emotional stars in Peter's life. As he says, "La Mare d'Auteuil! The very name has a magic, from all the associations that gathered round it during that time, to cling forever" (21). Passy thus affects the cast of Peter's mind but in the daily routine of his later life he exhibits the traits of a cultivated Englishman—his admiration of the English aristocracy (which leads him to trace his own ancestry back to the provincial French nobility), his love of manly sport such as boxing and swimming, his social snobbery, his conventional morality, and his love of British women, including his mother, Madame Seraskier, and the duchess of Towers.

The duality extends to Peter's name. Born Pierre Pasquier de la Marière, he is reborn in England as Master Peter Ibbetson. Along with his French name he must give up his individual dress and wear the gray coat of the Bluefriars' school—the price of becoming an English gentleman. There is, however, more than two names at stake here. Colonel Ibbetson, Peter's guardian, becomes for all practical purposes his surrogate father, and, as Peter later is led to believe, the colonel may be his true father. A rather sketchy villain, the colonel is said to have Jewish and colored blood in his veins. He enjoys hunting, which revolts Peter, is a reckless womanizer, affects the pose of a "swell" and is strikingly ugly. He is a grotesque parody of Peter's father and as such he is instinctively hated by Peter, who kills him and never once feels the slightest remorse.

It is notable that Peter's two fathers affect him in a way that is commensurate with the general pattern of the novel. "Le beau Pasquier," Peter's actual father, continues to live in Peter's dreamworld and is frequently visited in the still, beautiful garden of Passy. When he was a child, Peter would go to sleep while hearing his father sing: "Thus serenaded, I would close my eyes, and lapped in darkness and warmth and heavenly sound, be lulled to sleep—perchance to dream!" (29) His father survives like the song of Keats's nightingale in the "true dreams" for the remainder of Peter's life. Colonel Ibbetson, on the other hand, plays no part in Peter's inner life. Strictly excluded from the dream world, the colonel nevertheless greatly affects Peter's external existence: as guardian he makes Peter miserable and as victim he makes him a prisoner. The two fathers, then, stand opposed as dream and reality, song and cacophony, spirit and flesh, and life and death. There is no compromise between those extremes.

The splitting of the father figure into two distinct selves, one hated, the other admired, is an attractive fantasy. Such bifurcations of the mother figure are common in fairy tales, where an evil stepmother or witch stands opposed to a fairy godmother. The ambiguous attitude that a child may have toward his father or mother is thereby dealt with through a screening process that simplifies the ambiguity by dividing the parent into two personalities, one threatening and the other loving. Du Maurier thus presents an idealized version of his father in the character of "le beau Pasquier" and focuses all threatening and unpleasant traits in the character of Colonel Ibbetson. By having Peter murder the colonel, Du Maurier finally eliminates altogether the menacing aspects of the father. The fact that neither Peter's father nor Colonel Ibbetson are believable characters is precisely due to the bifurcation involved in this fantasy.

The theme of duality also involves the central women of the novel, Madame Seraskier, Madame Pasquier, and the duchess of Towers. Both the descriptions and illustrations reveal them to be nearly identical in beauty and stature. The "divine" Madame Seraskier is presented in terms of idealized beauty and a beauty associated with Peter's mother. She is some inches taller than his mother and, we are told, "my mother soon became the passionately devoted friend of the divine Madame Seraskier"(35). Like his mother she possesses warmth, kindness, simplicity, grace, naturalness, courtesy, sympathy, and joy. Despite her few inches and slight Irish accent, she is not easily distinguished from Peter's mother. It is not a total surprise, therefore, that they both die about the same time. The coincidence of their deaths is perhaps a too obvious continuance of the plot, but it has a certain psychological cogency. What appears to be involved here is the Oedipal wish to possess the mother without guilt by splitting the mother figure into the virgin and the sexual object. The bifurcation is more complicated in this instance than it is with the father figure. With the deaths of the idealized mother and the divine Madame Seraskier, Peter is free to fall in love with the duchess of Towers and to allow her to press her lips to his. The duchess of Towers is a composite figure: she is an allowable sexual object because she is sufficiently distanced from the mother, and yet her character includes the desirable traits of Peter's mother.

Mimsey Seraskier, meanwhile, emerges from her ungainly and sickly childhood to become the beautiful and flawless duchess of Towers, combining all of the virtues and loveliness of Mesdames Seraskier and Pasquier. The all-encompassing, intense, and spiritual relationship between Peter and the duchess is understandable in this light. In his dream, shortly after his sentence is commuted to life imprisonment, Peter meets the duchess in the garden at Passy and exclaims: "for the first time in my life since my mother and Madame Seraskier had died I held a woman in my arms, and she pressed her lips to mine" (294).

Finally, the most important thematic duality is that of Peter's mind itself, as he conducts his life for some thirty years on two levels, that of everyday consciousness and that of dreams. A hero with a fundamental division in his psyche or character was becoming a common one at this time. Robert Louis Stevenson's *The Strange Case of Dr. Jekyll and Mr. Hyde* (1886) and Oscar Wilde's *The Picture of Dorian Gray* (1890), for example, focus upon such a psychological theme. The duality in *Peter Ibbetson*, however, is not between good and evil, superego and id, but rather between dream and reality, with an almost compulsive emphasis that argues that dream *is* reality. The duality is more an aesthetic one than a moral one. Associated with Peter's dreams are childhood, unspoiled nature, songs, beautiful people, works of art and literature, freedom, and timelessness. In his waking life, on the other hand, there are ugly people (Colonel Ibbetson, Pentonville schoolmates, and prison inmates), ugly scenes (Pentonville), spoiled nature (the stumps of his childhood apple tree and the general destruction wrought by progress upon Passy), and imprisonment.

Lionel Stevenson sees Du Maurier's duality to be rooted in the Pre-Raphaelite movement: "The essential quality of Pre-Raphaelitsm was its contradictory merging of meticulously observed detail with idealized and symbolic themes." He goes on to conclude that "one cannot help feeling the special flavour of his novels has some kinship with the paintings of the Pre-Raphaelite Brotherhood and the poetry of Gabriel and Christina Rossetti. There may even be something specifically reminiscent of 'The Blessed Damozel' in the closing of *Peter Ibbetson*, when Mary comes back after her death to assure her lover that they will soon be united."[5] William Gaunt's observation about the Pre-Raphaelite world applies equally well to Du Maurier's novel:

it was real and unreal. . . . It was an escape from the age and a means of converting it. It was a circle in which the future and past chased each other round. It was a dimension, in which people and things were actual and yet phantom. Within its luminous boundary human lives were to assume . . . an inconsequent two-sidedness, on a plane or series of planes which were now in this world and now in this world of make-believe and at intervals, with a mixture of the jolliest farce and the strangest agony, in both worlds at once.[6]

The division between Peter's waking and dreaming lives may also owe something to Walter Pater. As Stevenson observes, "nowhere else in fiction is there so genuine an embodiment of the gospel that was proclaimed by Walter Pater. Both through the sensibilities of his characters and through his own inserted rhapsodies, Du Maurier is constantly seeking to convey to his readers the ecstasy of sensuous response to beauty."[7] Only in his dreams is Peter capable of fulfilling Pater's dictum: "To burn always with this hard, gem-like flame, to maintain this ecstasy, is success in life."[8] In this light one can understand Peter's comment at the end of the novel when he states that a cell in a criminal lunatic asylum has been to him like a bower in the Elysian Fields.

Telepathic Dreams

By "dreaming true" Peter is able to establish telepathic communication with the duchess of Towers. While something of a novelty, the idea of mental telepathy was not original with Du Maurier. In Benjamin Disraeli's *Contarini Fleming* (1832), Contarini and his beautiful Italian cousin discover that they were seeing one another in dreams before they met. Charlotte Bronte, in *Jane Eyre*, also employs the idea when she has Rochester call out for Jane in his misery. Over a hundred miles away, Jane hears his call. And Heathcliff, in Emily

Bronte's *Wuthering Heights*, is communicating with Catherine's spirit during his dying weeks. Du Maurier has taken this concept of telepathy between lovers and expanded it into an elaborate system that pervades a full half of the novel. The brief flashes of telepathy in the earlier novels never leave the reader with any doubt as to which is the real world. By making the narrator both a "madman" and a self-conscious practitioner of telepathy, Du Maurier brings the psychology of dreams to the forefront and makes it the substance of his novel.

Du Maurier's earliest vivid recollection from his childhood was not that of an actual experience but of a recurrent dream:

> I used to sleep in my parents' room, and when I turned my face to the wall, a door in the wall used to open, and a *charbonnier*, a coal-man, big and black, used to come and take me up and carry me down a long, winding staircase, into a kitchen, where his wife and children were, and treated me very kindly. In truth, there was neither door, nor *charbonnier*, nor kitchen. It was an hallucination; yet it possessed me again and again.[9]

His dream is transmuted in *Peter Ibbetson* as follows:

> For my early childhood was often haunted by a dream, which at first I took for a reality—a transcendent dream of some interest and importance to mankind, as as the patient reader will admit in time. But many years of my life passed away before I was able to explain and account for it.
>
> I had but to turn my face to the wall, and soon I found myself in company with a lady who had white hair and a young face—a very beautiful young face.
>
> Sometimes I walked with her, hand in hand—I being quite a small child—and together we would feed innumerable pigeons who lived in a tower by a winding stream that ended in a water-mill. It was too lovely, and I would wake. (30)

The reader later discovers that the beautiful white-haired woman is not an hallucination but Peter's grandmother, Jeanne de Boismorinel: "she had lived again in me whenever, as a child, I had dreamed that exquisite dream, I could now evoke her at will; and, with her, many buried memories were called out of nothingness into life" (354). This dream not only connects the past with the present but it also helps to relate the first part of the novel to the second.

The world of dreams and telepathy is also foreshadowed early in the novel when Mimsey and Gogo are playing in the garden: "She had a strange fancy that a pair of invisible beings, '*La fee Tarapatapoum*,' and '*Le Prince Charmant*' . . . were always in attendance upon us . . . and would protect us through life" (37). These invisible guardians turn out to be not mere creations of Mimsey's vivid imagination, but the adult versions of Mimsey and Gogo's dreaming selves: the duchess of Towers and Peter, who later in the novel frequently return to Passy where they lovingly watch over their youth. The violence that Mimsey's presentiment does to time and space looks toward the philosophic lecture the duchess gives Peter at the end of the novel, in which she tells him that "time and space mean just the same as 'nothing!'" (396).

Henry James, who had little patience for an uninspired treatment of the subject of dreams, believed that Du Maurier "has achieved the miracle of redeeming from its immemorial dreariness that dream world of the individual which, if it had not definitely succumbed to social reprobation, would still be the bugbear of the breakfast table." He concludes that the novel is "one of the most ingenious of all conceits," and that "we all know how wide a berth we usually give other people's dreams: but who has not been thankful for those of Gogo Pasquier and the Duchess Mimsey?"[10]

Lost Innocence

It has been suggested that Henry Vaughan's line, "Happy those early dayes! when I shin'd in my Angell-infancy," and William Wordsworth's metaphor of growing up, "Shades of the prison-house begin to close," summarize the central theme of the novel. A basic theme in literature, the irrevocable movement from innocence to experience was especially popular with William Blake and the poets of the early nineteenth century. They believed strongly in the power of the imagination to carry the feelings and wonder of childhood into adult life. Time is a paradoxical villain who, because he will destroy the paradise of youth, makes these early years most precious. It may be true, as Robert Frost has said, that "nothing gold can stay," but generations of writers, obsessed with their childhood, have done their best to preserve those golden days in their writing.

The early pages of *Peter Ibbetson* are among the most powerful evocations of a happy childhood in all literature. Henry James remarks on their appeal:

> Was there ever a more delightfully dusty haze, like the thick western air of a suburb at the drop of a summer's day, then the whole evocation of Peter Ibbetson's Anglo-Parisian childhood, all stories and *brioche*, and all peopled (save for the Prendergasts) with figures graceful, gentle, distinguished, musical, and enormously tall? Indefinitely amiable are all those opening pages, and a rare exhibition of the passion of reminiscence.[11]

The Passy of Louis Phillipe is brought to life with precise descriptions of its eighteenth-century buildings, the shops in the rue de la Pompe, the avenue through the park of La Muette, the pond christened the Mare d' Auteuil, and all the sights, smells, sounds, and textures that thrilled the young Gogo. The following descriptions of the comfort and security of his home after an afternoon outing captures the quality of these opening pages:

> And, once home, it was good, very good, to think how dark and lonesome and shivery it must be out there by the *mare*, as we squatted and chatted and roasted chestnuts by the wood fire in the school room before the candles were lit—*entre chien, et loup*, as was called the French gloaming—while Thérèse was laying the tea-things, and telling us the news, and cutting bread and butter; and my mother played the harp in the drawing room above; till the last red streak died out of the wet west behind the swaying tree-tops, and the curtains were drawn, and there was light, and the appetites were let loose. (47)

It never rains in Passy and the summer day on which the novel opens establishes the idyllic, enchanted atmosphere of these golden days: "It was on a beautiful June morning in a charming French garden, where the warm, sweet atmosphere was laden with the scent of lilac and syringa, and gay with butterflies, and dragon flies and humblebees" (9).

Peter is suddenly removed from this exuberant, sweet, seemingly timeless physical paradise upon the death of his parents. He is not only an orphan but an outcast. If Passy was heaven, then Pentonville is hell, and it is only a matter of time before literal shades of the prison-house begin to close upon the growing boy. When he revisits Passy some years later he discovers the brutality of time. The park where he used to play "was gone, cut up, demolished" and was cut through by a railroad. His old house is gone and only a fragment of his garden remains, the old apple tree having been reduced to a stump "that did duty for a rustic table." In short, he remarks that "twelve short years had effaced all memory of us" (189).

Both the destruction of the apple tree and the murder of Colonel Ibbetson suggest a sexual awareness or knowledge that is destructive of Peter's earlier naive bliss, but this is a theme that is not clearly developed. As his external, waking life becomes more restricted through his unhappy revisitation of Passy and through his subsequent prison sentence, he is tormented by a vision of two hideous dancing dwarfs. They represent the nightmare of an experiential hell, the world of time and death, that only the duchess of Towers can repel and replace with her liberating and heavenly powers of dreaming true. These dark figures he first saw in the flesh, while watching a parade in St. Cloud, having just come from his painful return to Passy: "Two little deformed and discarded-looking dwarfs, beggars, brothers and sisters, with large toothless gaps for mouths and no upper lips, began to dance" (196). Later that night they reappear to him in a terrifying nightmare that more than anything else in the novel conveys the horrid antithesis of the Edenic dream of Passy:

As I got near to the avenue gate, instead of the school on my left there was a prison; and at the door a little thick-set jailer, three feet high and much deformed jaileress no bigger than himself, were cunningly watching me out of the corners of their eyes, and toothlessly smiling. Presently they began to waltz together to an old, familiar tune, with their enormous keys dangling at their sides; and they looked so funny that I laughed and applauded. But soon I perceived that their crooked faces were not really funny; indeed, they were fatal and terrible in the extreme, and I was soon conscious that these deadly dwarfs were trying to waltz between me and the avenue gate for which

I was bound—to cut me off, that they might run me into the prison, where it was their custom to hang people on a Monday morning. (201)

This is a dream of the death of childhood. A school, associated with his youth and the Maison d' Education of Monsieur Saindou, is replaced by a prison. The dwarf jailors in turn possess the bodies of children but harbor the intentions of the most sinister adults. Unlike the dream children of Passy, they are ugly and marked by physical decay in their toothlessness. They have the power to confine and to kill. The sweet music of Peter's father and mother is here turned into a grotesque waltz, one that would lead him to his own death. Later, after he kills Colonel Ibbetson, and is awaiting the death sentence, Peter again dreams of the two dwarfs. He believes that they have got him at last and are butting at him sideways, "showing their toothless gums in a black smile, and poisoning me with their hot sour breath!" (271). These demons of his unconscious mind, hellish emblems of death and despair, do not, of course, prevail.

The movement from innocence to experience, heaven to hell, is complete in Peter's two nightmares, but the technique of dreaming true allows him the ultimate reprieve. Du Maurier makes youth perpetual in Peter's dreams. As James observed, "The reader who would fain ask himself how it is that our author's vision succeeds in being so blissfully exclusive, such a reader ends by perceiving, I think, that this is because it is intensely a vision of youth and of the soul of youth. Every thing and every one is not only beautiful for him; it is also divinely young."[12] During the twenty-five years that Peter and the duchess meet in their dreams they age only in real life; in their dreamworld they remain a constant twenty-eight years of age. They both are in their fifties when they die.

It is interesting to note at this point that Du Maurier himself did not "dream true." He made a number of significant changes in his richly autobiographical early chapters in order to shear away some of the uncongenial realities of his actual childhood and to make Passy a more complete wish-fulfilling dream. In both the descriptions and illustrations, for example, Peter is depicted as both tall (six feet) and powerful. In his fight with Boitard, the blacksmith, he demonstrates his physical superiority before an admiring crowd of onlookers. Du Maurier himself, of course, was several inches shorter than Peter, though he longed to be tall, and never enjoyed such a resounding public victory. As Ormond points out, "the description of the hero is a little larger than life, the day-dreams of an adolescent who sees himself as a unique super-being."[13] Ellen Du Maurier becomes "la belle Madame Pasquier," tall and beautiful, while the irresponsible Louis-Mathurin is described as "*le beau* Pasquier," "tall and comely to the eye." Du Maurier blots out the many disagreements between his parents, their financial anxiety and their frequent moving of the family from one house to another, to picture the Pasquiers living in comfort, peace, and security. The most important change in Du Maurier's revision of his early years is to make Peter an only child, the center of his parents' love and attention.

Madness

Peter's cousin-editor, Madge Plunkett, makes it clear in her introduction to the memoir that Peter "went suddenly mad" shortly after the death of the duchess of Towers, and "after his frenzy subsided, he remained for many days in a state of suicidal melancholia" (5). Then, one day, he arose apparently cured of all symptoms of insanity and remained so until his death. It was during the last year of his life, we are told, that he wrote his memoir. If we believe Peter and his dreams, his sudden "cure" is attributable to the visit of the duchess, who comes from the dead to inform Peter that they will be reunited after death. But Madge Plunkett notes the ambiguity of Peter's insanity: "There seems to have been a difference of opinion, or rather a doubt, among the authorities of the asylum as to whether he was mad after the acute but very violent period of his brief attack had ended." Madge is convinced "that he was no romancer, and thoroughly believed in the extraordinary mental experience he has revealed" (6). It seems clear, however, that for Du Maurier Peter is a romantic hero who, because he dares to dream and to ignore the worldly pursuits of his contemporaries, is judged to be mad. He is a man who lives in a rich world of fantasy, not unlike a poet or an artist.

Du Maurier apparently had written half of his novel before he decided to make his hero mad. When he arrived at the point where Peter discovers how to dream true he could find no easy way to keep the lovers apart, a separation he needed in order to keep the novel from becoming just another love story. In his frustration he even thought of burning the manuscript. Finally, he conceived the solution: "I'll make the hero mad. . . . That will put everything right."[14] This solution committed Du Maurier to a series of melodramatic episodes reminiscent of Tennyson's "Maud" and the Victorian theater, that culminated in the death of Colonel Ibbetson and the sentencing of Peter to life imprisonment.

By making Peter Ibbetson the narrator, Du Maurier maintains the ambiguity of his hero's madness. Like some of the "mad" speakers of Robert Browning's dramatic monologues, Peter is a true believer and justifies his thoughts and actions to himself and clearly wins our sympathy and understanding. We accept his dreams as quite possibly true and, like Madge Plunkett, we definitely believe that he believes in them.

Still, if Peter were to be portrayed by one of the prison guards he would unquestionably be seen as mad: withdrawn, uncommunicative, listless, given to excessive sleep, and with a history of violent behavior, the prisoner claims to have traveled into the past with a beautiful companion and, in his own words, which surely condemn him as mad, "we have hobnobbed with Montaigne and Rabelais, and been personally bored by Malherbe, and sat at Ronsard's feet . . ." (366). Is there any need to discuss his claim to have walked round and round under the Mammoth, to have sketched the living prehistoric creature firsthand?

Despite the conventions and the delicacy of Du Maurier's fantasy, the fact remains that his hero is obsessed with the past, prefers to dwell in dreams of imagined prettier days over the shabby, uncongenial present, that he gradually shuts out the actual world almost entirely from his thoughts. "A rare exhibition of the passion of reminiscence"—as James describes the early part of the novel—becomes by the end of the story an exhibition of reminiscence for its own sake. The hero could indeed be argued to be mad, to demonstrate the symptoms of schizophrenia, even if he never killed his uncle nor went to prison and the lunatic asylum.

With Peter as narrator, however, the question of his madness will remain moot. He is, perhaps, no more mad than the soul in Tennyson's "The Palace of Art," who withdraws from society in order to surround herself with a rich array of aesthetic delights. Du Maurier was obviously alluding to this poem when he depicts Peter and the duchess of Towers living in their exquisite dream home, "*Magna sed Apta*," which they can magically decorate with any art treasure they choose, even—ludicrously—with the entire Louvre! Peter, in fact, describes his new home as a "palace of art." Unlike Du Maurier, Tennyson implies in his poem that such aesthetic isolation from the real world leads to ennui, arrogance, and spiritual pride, and at the end of the work he has the soul leave the palace to return to the valley and more common values. Du Maurier felt more comfortable with the philosophy of *l'art pour l'art* than did the laureate, even though it is espoused by an apparent madman. Perhaps that is the point, that Peter appears mad only to those people of unrefined sensibilities, the crass purveyors of utilitarianism, technology, capitalism, and the other mundane ingredients that comprise the ugliness of late Victorian life that Du Maurier saw in Pentonville.

The Progression of Styles

By having his hero a "mad" man, much like Tennyson's narrator in "Maud," Du Maurier was free to employ a variety of styles to reflect Peter's changing mental states. The narrative exposition is straightforward, colloquial, written in short sentences, with occasional allusions, and the inevitable French phrase or sentence to capture a special mood or perception. The opening chapter, however, is a rich lyric celebration of childhood that abounds in detailed sensuous imagery. Across the street from Peter's first French home, for example, are "garden walls overtopped with the foliage of horse-chestnut, sycamore, acacia, and lime; and here and there huge portals and iron gates defended by posts of stone gave ingress to mysterious abodes of brick and plaster and granite, many shuttered, and embosomed in sun-shot greenery" (16). This chapter goes beyond the artist's visual perception by adding detail upon detail to re-create the experience of growing up in a dazzling small world that harmonizes all of the senses.

During his depressing stay in Pentonville Peter expounds upon his agnosticism and his style shifts from the lyrical to the asbstract, the sentences becoming longer and more complex:

> The awe-inspiring and unalterable conception that had wrought itself into my consciousness, whether I would or no, was that of a being infinitely more abstract, remote, and inaccessible than any the genius of mankind has ever evolved after its own image and out of the needs of its own heart—inscrutable, unthinkable, unspeakable; above all human passions, beyond the reach of any human appeal; One upon whose attributes it was futile to speculate— One whose name was *It*, not *He*. (124)

Ormond argues that "this passage of the novel becomes a platform for Du Maurier's own ideas, his agnosticism, his belief in natural selection and his conviction that cruelty is the only real vice" and that "these intellectual themes are unnecessary asides, which play no part in the development of the story."[15] Dull and uninspired as the prose of this chapter may be, it nevertheless mirrors a necessary stage in the development of the hero as he moves from his happy childhood recollections, derived from a variegated sensual and emotional world, to his first attempt as a young man to make sense of his life amid the depressing environment of Pentonville. The flat style, the lifeless sentences, the sudden loss of rich detail, all reflect a state of mind that will be highly receptive to the doctrine of "dreaming true."

Later in the novel Peter falls into an even stronger depression after he is put in prison and thinks that he has lost the ability to dream true and to be in the company of the duchess. Part 5 of the novel is cast in a stream-of-consciousness form in an attempt to capture the anxiety and near panic of the narrator as he imagines his execution. The sentences become short and choppy, the paragraphs (sometimes only a phrase long) are set off from one another by spaced periods, and French is readily exchanged with English:

> They pinion you, and you have to walk and be a man, and the chaplain exhorts and prays and tries to comfort. Then a sea of faces; people opposite, who have been eating and drinking and making merry, waiting for *you*! A cap

is pulled over your eyes—oh, horror! horror! horror! . . . "Hereux tambour-major de Sicile!" . . . "Il faut laver son linge sale en famille, et c'est ce que j'ai fait. Mais ça va me coûter cher!" . . . Would I do it all over again? Oh, let me hope, yes! (268−69)

The last chapter in the novel, in which the spirit of Mary Seraskier returns to Peter to inform him what life is like beyond death, contains an amalgam of the earlier styles. Peter quotes over twenty pages of fragments from her long monologue—set off by spaced periods—and these passages are lyrical and abstract. Mary's broken monologue is essentially a celebration of the world of spirit, reminiscent of the ideology of Thomas Carlyle and the Transcendentalists:

I have come to tell you that we are inseparable forever, you and I, one double speck of spinal marrow—"Philipschen!"—one little grain of salt, one drop. There is to be no parting for *us*. . . .

But not till you join me shall you and I be complete, and free to melt away in that universal ocean, and take our part as One, in all that is to be. (395−96)

The tone of this whole section is one of breathless joy combined with exasperation at the inadequacy of language to convey the nature of the spirit world that sustains the joy. Therein lies the problem with this section of the book. Du Maurier's joy in Passy is conveyed in very specific terms—the sights and sounds of the village, the singing of his father, and the comforting watchfullness of his beautiful mother. But he obviously has no sure details upon which to base his character's joy in eternity, a shadowy promise of bliss presented in a clichéd image of the "universal ocean." We are told that in eternity "everywhere in it is Life, Life, Life! ever renewing and doubling itself, and ever swelling that mighty river which has no banks!" (401−2). How much more convincing are the scenes from Passy, where we smell the lilac and syringa, hear the bumblebees, and feel the warm June air in the French garden.

The progression of styles in *Peter Ibbetson* reinforces the major theme of lost innocence and joy. No matter how much Mary Seraskier protests the joys of the afterlife, her style betrays her and Peter. As he moves further away from his childhood his language reflects his loss—it becomes starkly philosophical in Pentonville, fragmented and anxious in prison, and lyrical but abstract and hollow toward his death. The powerful imagery, the simplicity, and the quickened joyful tone of the early chapters stand for the reader and for the hero as a potent memory of a paradise lost.

The Characters

Du Maurier's strength as a writer lies in his ability to create a compelling fantasy. Most of his characters are drawn so as to sustain that fantasy and therefore bear little resemblance to actual people. The personality of Peter Ibbetson, for example, remains vague and inconclusive. We never see him from the angle of other characters and, as a narrator who is obsessed with his childhood and with an idealized love, he seldom reveals other aspects of his character. Indeed, there are no other aspects. As the central consciousness of the novel, Peter is the repository of fantastic dreams and a powerful nostalgia. Contrasting with the fantasy are such dark moments as Peter's depression in Pentonville, his philosophic doubts about free will, and his conflict with Colonel Ibbetson. Through his dream life, however, the hero transcends the actual world and achieves a lasting joy. Peter's character is a fascinating embodiment of Pre-Raphaelite romanticism. He is a man in love with a vision of the past and of an ideal beauty, and the duchess of Towers is the incarnation of that vision.

The duchess of Towers is an elusive, symbolic figure. As Mimsey, she was drawn as a charming, simple and solemn child, frail, in poor health, a lover of music, Byron, roast chestnuts, and small animals. A very believable Victorian child, she metamorphoses into the beautiful woman, an embodiment of Peter's mother, Madame Seraskier, and the ideal of timeless beauty. She is Peter's, not to mention Du Maurier's, Beatrice. She is the guide to Peter's past, the comfort of his present, and the hope of his future. A Victorian Saint, like Dante Gabriel Rossetti's Blessed Damozel, she extends the promise of romantic love to beyond death.

Some of the minor characters are drawn vividly and memorably in only a few pages. Like figures in an artist's sketch book, they help to flesh out the narrator's account of his colorful childhood. Peter's Latin teacher at M. Saindou's grammar school, is Mr. Slade, a Cambridge sizar stranded in Paris:

> We used to sit on the stone posts outside the avenue gate and watch for his appearance a certain distant corner of the winding street.
>
> With his green tail coat, his stiff shirt collar, his thick flat thumbs stuck in the armholes of his nankeen waist-coat, his long flat feet turned inward, his reddish mutton-chop whiskers, his hat on the back of his head, and his clean, fresh, blooming, virtuous, English face—the sight of him was not sympathetic when he appeared at last. (50)

Major Duquesnois, who in his youth joined an abortive attempt to invade France under the leadership of a "certain grim Pretender," lives across the street from Gogo in Passy and fills the young boy's mind with stories of French heroism in battle. Du Maurier refers to him as "an almost literal translation into French of Colonel Newcome" (24), a character from Thackeray's novel *The Newcomes*. Monsieur le Major was one of the genial hosts of Peter's childhood and when he later revisits Passy he comes by accident upon the old, stooped pensioner being led by a Sister of Charity. The scene is short but establishes a warm spot of joy mixed with pathos in the narrator's heart:

> It was a long time before I could give him an idea of who I was—Gogo Pasquier!
>
> Then after a while he seemed to recall the past a little.
>
> "Ha, Ha! Gogo—gentil petit Gogo!—oui—oui—l'exercice? Portez . . . arrmes! arrmes . . . bras? Et Mimsé? bonne petite Mimsé! toujours mal à la tête?"
>
> He could just remember Madame Seraskier; and repeated her name several times and said, "Ah! elle etait bien belle, Madame Seraskier!"
>
> In the old days of fairy-tale telling, when he used to get tired and I still wanted him to go on, he had arranged that if, in the course of the story, he suddenly brought in the word "Cric," and I failed to immediately answer "Crac" the story would be put off till our next walk (to be continued in our next!) and he was so ingenious in the way he brought in the terrible word that

I often fell into the trap, and had to forego my delight for that afternoon.

I suddenly thought of saying "Cric!" and he immediately said "Crac!" and laughed in a touching, senile way—"Cric! c'est bien ca!" and then he became quite serious and said—

"Je crains que monsieur ne le fatigue un peu!"

So I had to bid him good-bye. (190)

Most of Du Maurier's characters are from the middle or upper classes. He always admired the beautiful aristocracy, even in his early drawings for *Punch*. But Mr. Lintot, the architect to whom Peter is apprenticed, is a character right out of the novels of Dickens or the drawings of Charles Keene. His sympathy with the hero strengthens the fantasy of a childhood where naiveté is blessed. He quickly becomes Peter's friend, and teaches him to smoke and drink gin and water. Although he does his work well, sometimes he would drink more than was good for him and rave about Percy Shelley, "his only poet," and recite "Ode to a Skylark" with uncertain *h*'s and a rather cockney accent:

> 'Ail to thee blythe sperrit!
> Bird thou never wert,
> That from 'eaven, or near it
> Po'rest thy full 'eart
> In profuse strains of hunpremeditated hart. (85)

Du Maurier failed to make his villain, Colonel Ibbetson, convincingly evil, but his trial attempt at such a portrayal would bear fruit in his next novel with the powerful character of Svengali. The trouble with Colonel Ibbetson's villainy is that we are told about it instead of being made witnesses of it. To Du Maurier's credit, however, he did not reproduce the stock villain of melodrama but rather an ambiguous creature who, though repulsive, has a number of redeeming qualities. His physical appearance is grotesque because it is a composite of the gentleman and the savage: "this remote African strain still showed itself in Uncle Ibbetson's thick lips, wide-open nostrils, and big black eyes with yellow whites," but "in spite of his ugly face, he was not without a certain soldier-like air of distinction, being very tall and powerfully built" (83). And despite his reprehensible morality and his cruel treatment of his nephew, the colonel was a highly civilized and talented person. He could sketch, play the guitar, sing chansonettes and canzonets, write society verses, quote Alfred Musset, and knew several languages ("he had been an Eton boy"). But the mysterious strain of African and Semitic blood in his veins, Du Maurier seems to suggest, twists his character in the direction of villainy, even as Svengali's foreign blood helped to design his evil mind. As was pointed out earlier, the character of the colonel derives its emotional power from Du Maurier's fantasy that depicts him as a threatening father figure.

Edmund Wilson notes the dual role of the Jew in Du Maurier's novels and argues that he appears "in Colonel Ibbetson, Svengali in his ordinary relations—now as a malignant devil, whose malignancy is hardly accounted for; now—in Leah, Little Billee and the Svengali who animates Trilby—as a spirit from an alien world who carries with it an uncanny prestige, who may speak in a divine tongue."[16] In general terms Wilson's observation is perceptive, but he fails to see that even in the character of Colonel Ibbetson Du Maurier was revealing his paradoxical feelings about the Jew. The rough ambiguity of Colonel Ibbetson's character served as a model for the more carefully developed and complex character of Svengali.

The Illustrations

Since Du Maurier was a well-known artist, it was both obvious and wise for Harper's to request he illustrate his first novel, thereby combining the best of two talents into one. The eighty-four drawings proved to be more demanding to Du Maurier than the writing itself, but the painful care he gave to their execution was warmly acknowledged by James in a review essay in 1897:

[The drawings] are a part of the delicacy of the book and unique as an example of illustration at its happiest; not one's own idea, or somebody else's, of how somebody looked and moved or some image was constituted, but the lovely mysterious fact itself, precedent to interpretation and independent of it. The text might have been supplied to account for them. . . .[17]

The worlds of dream and reality are distinctively drawn, the dream scenes showing Peter and Mary as transparent figures against an idealized natural setting. Both Peter and Mary are very tall, handsome figures, impeccably dressed and genteel. There are many scenes of drawing rooms, restful gardens and lakes, and distinctive areas of England and France as a background for the characters. The close family groupings of the early chapters are in notable contrast to the Pentonville scenes, that show row houses, smoky skies, and near deserted streets. The family drawings fill a whole page whereas those of Pentonville are small quarter-page cuts. The theme of lost youth is brought out dramatically in the last few illustrations. Peter is drawn as a gaunt, wrinkled figure in a shabby rumpled suit. Mary, however, retains her elegance, though her hair has become white. Du Maurier's women are all drawn as tall, beautiful persons that age cannot tarnish. Madame Seraskier and her grown daughter are drawn to be almost identical, and Peter's mother, though half a head shorter than they, has very similar features. In contrast to these beautiful creatures there is Colonel Ibbetson, whose side-whiskers and piglike nose make him physically repulsive. The most grotesque drawing, however, is reserved for the two evil dwarfs who attempt to imprison Peter. The illustration is almost totally black, the only light coming from a distant street lamp that backlights the two dreadful dancing figures, whose eyes, noses, and broad grinning mouths are black holes. Peter stands startled in the left foreground, the dim outline of a gallows directly over his top hat.

The Romantic Tradition

In his essay "George Du Maurier and the Romantic Novel" Lionel Stevenson argues that the unprecedented popular appeal of Du Maurier's novels stems from his weaving both old and new strands of interest into an apparently casual texture: "Writing in the transitional decade of the nineties, he derived ingredients from the accumulated fiction of the whole nineteenth century, and instinctively combined them with currrent ideas that were to develop into the major innovations of the twentieth. [18] A few years before Du Maurier began writing *Peter Ibbetson*, there was a critical controversy raging over the respective merits of realism and romance. Henry James in his essay

"The Art of Fiction," published in *Longman's Magazine* in 1884, declared that realism is the aim and basis of great fiction: "The novel is in its broadest definition a personal, a direct impression of life: that, to begin with, constitutes its value . . ." and "the air of reality (solidity of specification) seems to me to be the supreme virtue of a novel. . . ."[19]

James's essay led Robert Louis Stevenson to write a series of articles in which he defended romantic fiction. He argus that "no art does 'compete with life.' Man's one method, whether he reasons or creates, is to half shut his eyes against the dazzle and confusion of reality." A novel, Stevenson insists, "is a work of art . . . not by its resemblances to life . . . but by its immeasurable difference from life, which is designed and significant, and is both the method and the meaning of the work."[20]

Oscar Wilde supported Stevenson's thesis in his essay "The Decay of Lying" (1889), in which he writes: "The ancient historians gave us delightful fiction in the form of fact; the modern novelist presents us with dull facts under the guise of fiction. . . . He has not even the courage of other people's ideas, but insists on going directly to life for everything." Wilde laments how the young, born with a natural gift for exaggeration, fall into "careless habits of accuracy" and develop "a morbid and unhealthy faculty of truth-telling" until he writes novels that are "so like life that no one can possibly believe in their probability."[21]

While subsequent critical opinion sided with James that the psychological, objective novel of character was superior to the romantic novel, the vast majority of the reading public continued to prefer the latter. Beginning about 1886 the school of romantic fiction dominated the literary scene. Rider Haggard published *King Solomon's Mines*, *She*, and *Allan Quatermain* between 1886 and 1888. Sir Arthur Conan Doyle contributed *A Study in Scarlet*, *The Sign of the Four*, *The Adventures of Sherlock Holmes*, and *The White Company* between 1887 and 1891. Quiller-Couch wrote *Dead Man's Rock*, *Troy Town*, and *The Splendid Spur* between 1887 and 1889. Stanley Weyman reinvigorated historical fiction with *The House of the Wolf*, *A Gentleman of France*, and *Under the Red Robe* between 1889 and 1894. Anthony

Hope created a new romantic theme with *The Prisoner of Zenda* in 1894.

All of these authors were at the peak of their careers when Du Maurier was writing and his three novels clearly follow the stream of romantic fiction then in vogue. But, as Lionel Stevenson points out, "he adapted the attributes of the romantic tradition to suit the mood of a new epoch." Du Maurier introduced the idea of the mysterious powers of the human psyche and "employed the abnormal accomplishments of the conscious and the unconscious mind for a purpose totally different from that which earlier writers of supernatural fiction had striven for."[22] Du Maurier eschewed terror and suspense and provided his readers instead with the gratification of seeing a talented individual overcome ordinary human limitations.

Du Maurier chose not to follow the characteristic feature of the romantic novel of having a setting remote in time and place. Instead he set his characters in England and France. Nevertheless, as he points out in his novels, the Paris of the Citizen King and the second republic had disappeared as irrevocably as the Pharaohs. Henri Murger in *Scénes de la Vie de Bohème* (1847–49) had already painted a glamorous picture of bohemian life in the Paris of Louis Philippe. The period was soon perceived by the English public as an exotic one, and, in 1890, Du Maurier was able to write firsthand accounts of a country and a time that his readers considered romantically remote.

Despite Peter Ibbetson's ability to "dream true," as a character he is different from the hero of romantic fiction who is typically a rugged explorer, a swashbuckling swordsman, or a master-mind of criminal detection. Peter Ibbetson is an unsuccessful architect. Outside of murdering his uncle, he does very little to change the physical world he inhabits. He is not a man of action, but possesses an innate sort of heroism: he is unselfish, modest, chivalrous, courageous, and physically handsome.

The most notable feature of *Peter Ibbetson*, indeed, of all Du Maurier's novels, that mark it as romantic fiction is that it is filled with his own personality made larger than life. As Lionel Stevenson observes, "His digressive comments, his emotional versatility—abruptly shifting from humour to pathos, from satire to sympathy—gave the flavour of his personality to every page."[23] Although it is an intensely personal novel it embodies a universal theme. In the words of Deems Taylor, who turned the novel into an opera in 1931, Du Maurier's tale is "the Freudian Wish expressed in terms of romance, our rebellious human hope of a world more enjoyable than the one we live in, our flight into dreams, wherein we can find sanctuary from a waking life that is, on the whole, a disappointment."[24]

"ET MAINTENANT DORS, MA MIGNONNE!"
Svengali hypnotizes Trilby.

Chapter Four
Trilby

The Influence of Murger

Reviewing the play *Trilby*, the usually waspish George Bernard Shaw enthusiastically announced that he greatly enjoyed reading the novel: "It is a homogeneous work of art in which the master, like a composer who sets his own poem to music, shows us his people by the art of the draughtsman, and tells us their story by the art of the fabulist."[1] Henry James, in an essay on Du Maurier's life and works, records that "it was not till the first installment of *Trilby* appeared that we really sat up."[2] Not only did demanding and sophisticated critics like Shaw and James sit up and take notice, but the public at large became so fascinated by this story about a French working girl and her mysterious hypnotist lover that in major cities in both England and America the book quickly became the number one best-seller with nearly 300,000 copies sold by the end of 1894, its first year of publication.

Some of the success of the novel clearly derives from its exotic subject matter. Du Maurier gives the reader an inside look at the lives of three young English artists, Little Billee, the Laird, and Taffy, studying painting in Paris and adapting to bohemian life in the Latin Quarter. They meet the charming and beautiful young Trilby, who has modeled in the nude ("the altogether," as Du Maurier phrases it), and whose lack of chastity is compensated for by her simple energy and charm. Little Billee falls in love with Trilby, refuses to take her as his mistress, and asks her to marry him, but his even more prudish mother intervenes to persuade Trilby that marriage would ruin her son's chance to become a famous artist. In an act of nobility Trilby vanishes from the scene, and Little Billee, after going through a period of depression, emerges from his despair as a successful artist in London. Trilby, meantime, to the surprise of both the reader and Little Billee, has become the lover of the sinister Svengali under whose hypnotic spell she gained international fame as the singer known as "La Svengali." Little Billee and his two friends come to Paris to attend her performance and are amazed at the transformation. Later they meet her in the Place de la Concorde, but mysteriously she does not appear to know who they are.

When she gives another performance in London, the three artists are again in attendance and observe Svengali glaring down at them from his box. His hatred for these three is so intense (for they were once all close to Trilby and represent a threat to his possession of her) that it leads to his death from a heart attack. Without the hypnotic control of Svengali, Trilby suddenly loses her singing ability and wakes as from a dream almost totally unaware of her past life. Her spirit weakened and abused, she dies a few days later surrounded by her three old friends from the Latin Quarter. Little Billee, broken-hearted, dies soon after. Taffy later comes to learn the whole story about Svengali's hypnotic control over Trilby and the life they led together, and with this account of Trilby's mysterious past the novel ends.

The chief literary source for Du Maurier's novel is Henri Murger's *Scènes de la Vie de Bohème* (1845), the basis of Puccini's famous opera *La Bohème*. Murger's work is comprised of several loose, episodic chapters that detail the romantic joys and depressions of several French students living in the Latin Quarter during the 1840s: Rudolphe, the poet, Marcel, the painter, Colline, the philosopher, and Schaunard, the musician. Spurning the bourgeois values of their day, these enterprising bohemians so delight in their poverty, their camaraderie, and their artistic literary talents that their youthful energy and playful movement throughout the cultural capital of Europe make their rootless lives appear both glamorous and exciting—despite the mundane realities of their squalid apartments and constant impoverishment. They freely rejoice in their talents, their lively talks over wine, and their evanescent love affairs. The strong bond between these young men finally weakens after some of them fall in love. The focus upon the tragic affair between Rudolphe and Mimi clearly demonstrates this divisive quality of love as Rudolphe withdraws from his friends to devote his energies to this spirited but fatally ill beauty. After her death both Rudolphe and his closely knit group of friends are changed and their bohemian paradise becomes more a memory than a reality. The story ends with Mimi's death and the reader is left with a pleasant melancholy—like that of the self-indulgent Rudolphe—and one is spared the story of his later life where, one fears, he would exchange his youthful bravado and idealism for middle-class acceptance and conventionality. *Scènes*, after all, is the story of youth and ends, appropriately, with the death of youth.

Du Maurier confided in his friend Luke Ionides that his novel was strongly indebted to the *Scènes de la Vie de Bohème*, "only the British public does not know that."[3] The similarities between the two works are clear enough: both focus upon a small group of talented youth living in the bohemian Latin Quarter during the middle of the century, and both feature a love affair—Mimi and Rudolphe; Trilby and Little Billee—that melodramatically ends in death. But while Murger's story is an obvious literary source for *Trilby*, it may have been a more important influence upon the life that Du Maurier actually lived when he was an art student in Paris. Possibly here is a case of life imitating art and then art imitating the amalgam of the two in the form of *Trilby*. It would be difficult to say how much of the idea for "the three musketeers of the brush" derives from Murger and how much from Du Maurier's firsthand experience in Paris.

Du Maurier's middle-class English morality gives his story a very different tone from Murger's. Murger's characters are truly bohemians. They are amoral and delight in flaunting the conventions of their day. Marriage is to be avoided and sex is to be pursued and enjoyed as a free, guiltless pleasure. Murger's lovers enjoy idyllic relationships that eschew deep commitments and social and economic realities. Their affairs are romantic fantasies, delightful and evanescent. Little Billee, on the other hand, embodies a rigid moral code and is a downright prude. He is shocked to discover that Trilby has posed in "the altogether" and is horrified at seeing her in the nude. Refusing to accept Trilby as his mistress, and losing the chance to marry her, Little Billee remains a virgin to his death. Du Maurier focuses most of the sexuality in this novel upon two things: Trilby's famous foot, which, in paintings, sculptures, and in the flesh is adored by Little Billee and her other admirers; and upon the relationship between Svengali and Trilby.

The Demonic Mesmerist

The structure of *Trilby* is similar to that of Du Maurier's other novels. The first part deals with the autobiographical details of the author's early days—in this instance, his years as an art student in Paris. Based on actual experiences and rendered in colorful detail, the opening chapters have the credibility of a memoir. The second part of the novel, however, turns from memoir to melodrama and fantasy as the story unfolds of a sinister hypnotist's deadly control over a French grisette. Having carefully established a realistic setting and believable characters, Du Maurier introduces the popular subject of hypnotism and turns the novel in the direction of fantasy and pseudo-science: the tone-deaf Trilby, under Svengali's hypnotic control, is transformed into the most famous and talented singer in all Europe.

The two sections of the novel are connected by the narrative, both Trilby and Svengali having appeared in the earlier sections. But Svengali's ominous powers are merely hinted at in the first part. It is only after Trilby disappears for a period of five years and we are into the last quarter of the novel that we discover Trilby's magical transformation and Svengali's full powers. Our suspicions about Svengali are generated throughout the believable chapters and confirmed in the fantastic ones. A sinister and mysterious creature when he is present, capable of evoking our fears and disgust, Svengali's powers grow in our imaginations during his long absence from the novel, and his subsequent reappearance as the devil-god manipulator and transformer of the innocent Trilby does not, after all, seem incredible at this point, but rather it mirrors and shapes our own imaginings.

Of all the themes in this novel, the one of hypnotic control of a subject is clearly the most dramatic and compelling. When Du Maurier's friend Moscheles was experimenting with mesmerism in Antwerp, in 1859, it was a relatively new phenomenon. Originally called animal magnetism by its discoverer, Franz Anton Mesmer, in 1779, the practice and theory of mesmerism entered England in the early 1800s. It was not until the 1840s, however, that public interest about mesmerism became aroused. A man named John Elliotson, the founder of the London Phrenological Association, was chiefly responsible for the "mesmeric mania" that swept England in the 1840s and after. The subject was treated in popular books, pamphlets, articles, lectures, and demonstrations. The experts made clear that great mental energy, sustained concentration of the will, is necessary to control its influence. The public quickly perceived that the three, characteristically Victorian powers—energy, will, and power—are potentially both destructive and constructive. The power of the mesmerist over his subject could lead to results that would harm both his subject and society at large. Some people feared the power would be used by an immoral leader for his own selfish ends. Others saw it as a magic power to cure everything from boredom to disease. It was in short, a fascinating and ambiguous power, awaiting either a god or a devil to wield it.[4]

Writers of sensational fiction gradually began to pick up on the idea of having their villains employ hypnotism to further their evil designs. Du Maurier himself illustrated two such stories for *Once a Week* in 1861 and 1862: "The Notting Hill Mystery" and "The Poisoned Mind." The latter, by A. G. G., may have suggested the theme of *Trilby*. It is a story about a sinister foreigner whose lover deserts him to marry a scientist. The foreigner contrives an ingenious plot in order to seek revenge upon the woman. He hypnotizes her so that she carries out scientific experiments, the significance of which she is ignorant. Her scientist husband, baffled by her behavior, desperately attempts to grasp the meaning of her experiments. His quest for that knowledge finally leads him to murder his wife who, of course, was unable to explain what she never knew and so the foreigner achieves his revenge.

These crude and rather mechanical thrillers are a far cry from the powerful theme that Du Maurier developed in *Trilby*. In his account of Svengali's domination of Trilby Du Maurier employs the daring theme of sexual domination. One of the great anxieties among Victorian critics of hypnotism arose from a sense of the potential danger of one person holding concentrated power over another. An immoral mesmerist, it was feared, could dominate a vulnerable, submissive subject. According to Fred Kaplan, the implicit anxiety was a sexual one: "The power to usurp the other's will was seen as inseparable from sexuality, the assumption being that the strongest male drive is the desire to succeed in fulfilling sexual needs often with an unwilling or resisting partner."[5] This may be one reason why Svengali, like Bram Stoker's Dracula, had such a powerful appeal to a reading public conditioned by Mrs. Grundy, and it may also be partly for this reason that the character of Svengali survives to this day.

The most significant predecessor of Svengali is the character of John Jasper in Charles Dickens's *The Mystery of Edwin Drood*, published in 1870. Fascinated with the subject of mesmerism, Dickens portrays in this novel a mysterious opium addict who appears to have hypnotic control over his beautiful young music pupil, Rosa Bud. The following passage demonstrates the remarkable similarity between Jasper's relationship to Rosa Bud and Svengali's relationship to Trilby. Rosa explains her terrible fear of and attraction to her mentor:

He has made a slave of me with his looks. He has forced me to understand him, without his saying a word; and he has forced me to keep silence, without his uttering a threat. When I play, he never moves his eyes from my hands. When I sing, he never moves his eyes from my lips. When he corrects me, and strikes a note, or a chord, or plays a passage, he himself is in the sounds, whispering that he pursues me as a lover, and commanding me to keep his secret. I avoid his eyes, but he forces me to see them without looking at them. Even when a glaze comes over them (which is sometimes the case), and he seems to wander away into a frightful sort of dream in which he threatens most, he obliges me to know it, and to know that he is sitting close at my side, more terrible to me then than ever.[6]

Rosa's attitude toward Jasper is clearly ambivalent and suggests her suppressed sexual attraction toward him. His strange psychic powers have made her his slave and threaten to release her erotic feelings.

Du Maurier introduces the theme of sexual domination in the early chapters of *Trilby*, when Svengali repeatedly boasts about his conquest of a woman named Honorine. What honor she may have had is now long gone, having been reduced to "a dirty, drabby little dolly-mop of a Jewess, a model for the figure."[7] Her first encounter with Svengali is described in sexual terms: "She went to see him in his garret, and he played to her, and leered and ogled, and flashed his bold, black beady Jew's eyes into hers, and she straightway mentally prostrated herself in reverence and adoration before this dazzling specimen of her race" (62).

Honorine was too easy game for Svengali and he loses interest in her. It is Trilby that he must have, and in one of his early encounters with her he delivers a bizarre sexual canticle to her body:

"Will you permit that I shall look into your mouth, matemoiselle?"
She opened her mouth wide, and he looked into it.
"Himmel! the roof of your mouth is like the dome of the Pantheon; there is room in it for 'toutes les glories de la France,' and a little to spare! The entrance to your throat is like the middle porch of St. Sulpice when the doors are open and not one tooth is missing—thirty-two British teeth as white as milk and as big as knuckle-bones! and your little tongue is scooped out like the leaf of a pink peony, and the bridge of your nose is like the belly of a Stradivarius—what a sounding-board! and inside your beautiful big chest the lungs are made of leather! and your breath, it embalms—like the breath of a beautiful white heifer fed on the buttercups and daisies of the Vaterland! and you have a quick, soft, susceptible heart, a heart of gold, matemoiselle—all that sees itself in your face!" (72)

The architectural and musical metaphors render her body as an object, an expensive and sacred one, but still an object. Her mouth and throat are entrances to an exotic temple. Her lungs are compared to a bellows and her nose to the finest-made violin. He thus implies that she is an exquisite instrument that can be played—not by herself, for she is tone-deaf—but by a master player like himself. This sacred temple is threatened by the possible entrance of the Jewish infidel. The exotic instrument will yield its music under the hands of the maestro. The passage is grotesque and beautiful at once, as Svengali mixes peonies and buttercups with knuckle-bones and heifers. The accompanying illustration, like the prose, has even the suggestion that he is examining Trilby as one might a horse before purchasing it: "thirty-two British teeth!"

Even though it is Trilby's mouth that he is inspecting, Trilby has a haunting fear of being devoured by Svengali: "He reminds me of a big hungry spider, and makes me feel like a fly!" All that day she carried "the memory of Svengali's big eyes and the touch of his soft, dirty finger-tips on her face; and her fear and her repulsion grew together" (75). One of Du Maurier's illustrations depicts a spider with Svengali's head sitting in the center of its web. The Victorian reader might well be reminded of Mary Howitt's famous verse, "'Will you walk into my parlour,' said the spider to the fly?" Again, the theme of sexual domination is underscored in the relationship between the large hungry spider and the trapped, defenseless fly. Svengali devours her with his eyes and desecrates her with his touch. His touch, like his body, is dirty, physically and morally. Much is made of the fact that Little Billee, the Laird, and Taffy take frequent baths and that Svengali mocks them for their concern for their cleanliness. But despite the repulsion Trilby feels for Svengali, she apparently feels a powerful attraction toward him that makes her afraid. It is the very fact that once one enters the spider's parlor she will not come out again that makes the room so fascinating and the threshold so tempting and yet so terrible to cross.

Svengali deliberately associates in Trilby's mind the subjects of love and death, and outdoes Andrew Marvell's "To His Coy Mistress" in his macabre seduction attempts to win Trilby's favor. Only half playfully he tells her that one day he will become famous and that by rejecting him now she will consign herself to poverty and finally take her own miserable life:

one fine day you shall lie asleep on one of those slabs—you, Drilpy, who would not listen to Svengali, and therefore lost him! . . . And over the middle of you will be a little leather apron, and over your head a little brass tap, and all day long and all night the cold water shall trickle, trickle all the way down your beautiful white body to your beautiful white feet till they turn green, and your poor, damp, draggled, muddy rags will hang above you from the ceiling for your friends to know you by; drip, drip, drip! But you will have no friends. (112)

Svengali fails to turn her head with these musings, and in a later meeting with her contrives an even more morbidly grotesque seduction:

what a beautiful skeleton you will make! . . . You shall have a nice little mahogany glass case all to yourself in the museum of the École de Médecine, and Svengali shall come in his new fur-lined coat smoking his big cigar of the Havana, and push the dirty carabins out of the way, and look through the holes of your eyes into your stupid empty skull, and up the nostrils of your high, bony sounding-board of a nose without either a tip or a lip to it, and into the roof of your big mouth, with your thirty-two big English teeth, and between your big ribs into your big chest, where the big leather lungs used to be, and say, "Ach! What a pity she had no more music in her than a big tomcat!" And then he will look all down your bones to your poor crumbling feet, and say, "Ach! What a fool she was not to answer Svengali's letter!" (135—36)

In the morgue scenario, Svengali undresses Trilby to reveal the pointless waste of her fine white flesh. But here, in the museum scenario, he unfleshes her with his eyes and alludes to his initial inspection of her mouth but now displaces the grand images of the Pantheon and St. Sulpice with those of emptiness and hollowness. Aggressive and hostile in his tone, Svengali, in his three speeches, has examined the body of Trilby in stages that are successively more macabre and punishing: the bizarre praise of her mouth, throat, chest, and lungs, followed by the image of her naked white body turning green in the morgue, climaxed by a penetrating survey of the hollows of her skeleton in the museum. Like the spider with which Trilby has associated him, he has proved his hunger by devouring his victim and picking her bones clean. It is small wonder that Trilby perceived him as a "dread, powerful demon, who . . . oppressed and weighed on her like an incubus—and she dreamed of him oftener than she dreamed of Taffy, the Laird, or even Little Billee!" (136—37). An incubus is a demon believed to descend upon sleeping women with whom they have sexual relations, and the simile in the quoted passage is directly relevant to the theme of the novel. The fact that Trilby has recurrent dreams about Svengali singles him out from the proper and prudish Englishmen as a potent, dreadful, all-devouring sexual force, more appropriate to Victorian nightmares than to rational discourse. The foreigner is rousing sexual feeling that is already present, but repressed. What Trilby fears is the arousal of this latent female sexuality.

After the passage of five years we see the new Svengali, rich and powerful, and Trilby, a famous singer. Significantly, she is now known as "La Svengali." Under her lover's hypnotic spell, she has become an extension of him, totally possessed by his spirit: "Trilby was just a singing-machine—an organ to play upon—an instrument of music—a Stradavarius—a flexible flageolet of flesh and blood—a voice, and nothing more" (458). Svengali's henchman, Gecko, who fills in the story of Trilby's transformation during her five years' absence, says that Svengali "used to work Trilby too hard; it was killing her—it killed her at last. And then at the end he was unkind to her and scolded her and called her names—horrid names"(453). The strong sexual implications in Svengali's earlier speeches have now reached fruition in aesthetic terms. Trilby has become a singing-machine that he plays to perfection and through which he achieves recognition, wealth, and power.

Up to this point, Svengali's story is like that of a fairy tale, in which the possession of a magical power allows one to fulfill his dreams. But here, hypnotism, and the implicit theme of sexual domination, not only leads to fulfilled dreams but also to death and destruction. The moral structure of the novel demands the punishment of Svengali (he dies and is renounced by his henchman, Gecko, as a cruel and ruthless tyrant) and the apotheosis of Trilby. As Gecko explains, *"There were two Trilbys.* There was the Trilby you knew. . . . She was an angel in paradise. She is now! . . . But all at once—pr-r-r-out! presto! augenblick! . . . with one wave of his hand over her—with one look of his eye—with a word—Svengali could turn her into the other Trilby, *his* Trilby—and make her do whatever he liked" (458). One Trilby may have been violated, used, and finally destroyed by the demon-incubus, but the other Trilby remains the sweet angel of Paradise she always was. Sex and death are related in Svengali's speeches to Trilby, and his long domination of her body finally leads to their deaths forming the climax of their relationship and of the novel.

The subtheme of duality, the two Trilbys, allows Du Maurier a moral and romantic conclusion. Trilby's sexuality remains suppressed so as not to threaten her three male friends. As in *Dracula*, there is present in this novel a fear of female sexuality, and Trilby's erotic self emerges only under the hypnotic influence of Svengali. The two Trilbys are similar to the twins, Laura and Lizzie, in Christina Rossetti's "Goblin Market." Laura falls under the sexual spell of the malicious, seductive goblin men but Lizzie remains always pure. Du Maurier had already developed the theme of duality in *Peter Ibbetson*, and here again creates a character living two separate lives. But while Peter's "dreaming true" liberated and brought him a new life, Trilby's trance-life enslaved her and caused her early death. After Svengali dies and her spell is broken Trilby exclaims, "It all seems like a bad dream! What was it all about? *Was* it a dream, I wonder?" (388).

The Demonic Orpheus

Du Maurier fuses the theme of mesmerism with that of music and thereby adds a paradoxical quality to the power and influence of Svengali. Music plays a large part in Du Maurier's novels, even as it did in his life, but nowhere is the subject more in evidence than in *Trilby*. By depicting Svengali as a virtuoso, Du Maurier dramatizes Shakespeare's observation that "music oft hath such a charm / To make bad good, and good provoke to harm."

Despite his villainy, Svengali's musical credentials and talent are impressive: "He had but one virtue—his love of his art; or, rather, his love of himself as a master of his art—*the* master. . . . He had been the best pianist of his time at the Conservatory in Leipsec" (58). Du Maurier, however, limits the heavenly aesthetic heights to which he allows this demon-musician to ascend: "He had to draw the line just above Chopin, where he reached his highest level. It will not do to lend your own quite peculiar individual charm to Handel and Bach and Beethoven; and Chopin is not bad as a *pis-aller*." Nevertheless, Svengali's music is repeatedly associated with heaven and the divine. He can make "unheard heavenly melody of the cheapest, trivialest tunes," and playing Chopin on the pianoforte he appeared "as one of the heavenly host" (59).

The literary tradition of the fabulous powers of music goes back centuries. There are the mythological figures of Arion, Amphion, the Sirens, Marsyas and Linus, and the predominate personage of Orpheus himself. The music of Orpheus' lyre was so beautiful that when he played, wild beasts were soothed, trees danced, and rivers stood still. In the Orphic tradition music was depicted as not only something beautiful and harmonious within itself but as an extension of one's powers and mastery over the unruly world. With the creation of the character of Svengali, Du Maurier introduces a sinister element to the

Orphic theme. Through his combined mastery of music and hypnotism, Svengali can control Trilby—and through her song control the minds and hearts of thousands of people throughout Europe. Power becomes an end in itself and the vital medium for this power is the voice of Trilby, through which Svengali expresses himself.

Du Maurier makes it clear that Svengali himself was "absolutely without voice, beyond the harsh, hoarse, weak raven's croak he used to speak with, and no method availed to make one for him" (58). Upon examining the mouth of Trilby—the mouth that will one day obey his commands and sing beautifully, Svengali employs several musical metaphors noted earlier: "the bridge of your nose is like the belly of a Stradivarius—what a sounding board! and inside your big beautiful chest the lungs are made of leather." He will perfect and play upon this human instrument and, like Orpheus' lyre, its music will enchant the world.

In a comparison between painting and music, Svengali argues convincingly that music exerts a more far-reaching influence on and control over one's audience, a mastery well suited to his demonic ego that would rule the world:

When his [Little Billee's] little fool of a picture is finished he will send it to London, and they will hang it on a wall with a lot of others, all in a line, like recruits called out for inspection, and the yawning public will walk by in procession and inspect, and say "damn!" Svengali will go to London *himself*. Ha! Ha! He will be all alone on a platform, and play as nobody else can play; and hundreds of beautiful Englanderinnen will see and hear and go mad with love for him—Prinzessen, Comtessen, Serene English Altessen. They will soon lose their Serenity and their Highness when they hear Svengali. (109)

He goes on to picture the aristocracy enraptured by his rendition of Chopin and later sitting all around him on footstools, bringing him tea and gin and cookies. For Svengali, music, like mesmerism, is power and control. It enables him to transcend his social and economic rank and reach a point where the aristocracy of England serve him, a poor Jewish foreigner.

When Little Billee first hears of "La Svengali" from another famous singer, her voice is described in terms of an instrument: "Everything that Paganini could do with his violin, she does with her voice—only better . . ." (258). Legend had it that the only way Paganini could have achieved his virtuosity on the violin was by selling his soul to the devil.[8] Du Maurier's association of Svengali with the devil is subtly reinforced through this allusion. Svengali is the real virtuoso and Trilby merely his angelically tuned instrument. Her performance at Paris, where Little Billee first realizes that "La Svengali" is Trilby, is mesmeric and demonstrates the awesome power of music over its listeners. Svengali as conductor controls the entire production. He taps his baton and the overture is described as a "strange seduction" and an "enchantment," terms appropriate to its hypnotic effect. Trilby's voice is described in similar language: "the seduction, the novelty of it, the strangely sympathetic quality!" (318). The narrator comments further that "you did not require to be a lover of music to fall beneath the spell of such a voice as that" (323). And Théophile Gautier, in a supposed review of Trilby's performance, writes that "one need not have a musical ear . . . to be enslaved by such a voice as hers." Svengali's demonic power controls Trilby and is transformed through her into a musical form of angelic beauty. Gautier asks if she is "Ange, ou Femme?" (333). And the narrator observes that only "a woman archangel might sing like that" (320). As an extension of Svengali's own power and musicality, Trilby is appropriately renamed "La Svengali," and her description as an "archangel" reflects her lover's Satanic nature. At her final performance, during which Svengali loses control over her and her singing voice fails, there is this interesting exchange between Trilby and Monsieur J., the conductor taking Svengali's place:

> "But sing then, madame—for the love of God, begin, begin!"
> "How in the devil do you expect me to sing with all the noise they are making, those diabolic musicians!"
> "But, my God, madame—what do you want then?" cried Monsieur J——.
> "It's just that I prefer singing without all that Satanic music!" (376)

The references to God, the devilish musicians and the Satanic music further strengthen the relationship between Svengali's demonic character and the music. During the excited exchange between Trilby and the frustrated conductor, Svengali is seen "smiling a ghastly, sardonic smile, a rictus of hate and triumphant revenge" (379). No longer under his control, she senses that the music and the musicians are demonic, and fails to sing. The audience, in turn, responds with "shouts of laughter, hoots, hisses, catcalls, cock-crows" (378). With the death of the demonic mesmeric Orpheus, there is no music, and both Trilby and the audience go out of control and the theater is reduced to tumult and pandemonium.

The Corruption of Innocence

There is another important theme in this novel, one that is over-shadowed by the more powerful themes of mesmerism and music, although connected to them: the loss of innocence and youth. Du Maurier developed this theme in *Peter Ibbetson* and now traces it through the characters of Little Billee and Trilby. Henry James notes the recurrence of this theme through all of Du Maurier's novels: "We find ourselves constantly in contact with the beautiful unhappy young. . . . They are happy, of course, at the start; there would else be no chance for the finer complication. . . . I like best his touch for the pains and the penalties. His feeling for life and fate arrives at a bright, free, sensitive, melancholy utterance."[9] *Trilby* unfolds a tale of lost youth, lost love, lost innocence, and lost opportunity. It is precisely the evanescent quality of the youthful joys and loves that invests them with their great value. As Wallace Stevens put it, in "Sunday Morning," "Death is the mother of beauty."

The early chapters of *Trilby* establish a romantically idealized world in which "the three musketeers of the brush" are completely at home: "Oh, happy days and happy nights, sacred to art and friend-ship! Oh, happy times of careless impecuniosity, and youth and hope and health and strength and freedom—with all Paris for a play-ground, and its dear old unregenerate Latin quarter for a workshop and a home" (41). This world derives its solidity from the strong male bond between Little Billee, Taffy, and the Laird. When Trilby first enters the life of the three artists she brings them even more closely together and they seem almost a family. "In the caressing, demonstra-tive tenderness of her friendship," we are told, "she 'made the soft eyes' at all three indiscriminately" (97). Theirs is a very chaste arrangement in which Trilby, when she is not serving the three as an inspiring model, assumes the traditional role of a Victorian housewife: "she dearly loved her own way, even in the sewing on of buttons and the darning of socks" (96). It is quite striking that the males bond, as in *Dracula*, to protect Trilby, a mother figure, and to keep the foreigner from arousing her sexuality. They want to keep her as a mother figure, and their suppression of her sexuality suggests that there may be an Oedipal fantasy at work here.

But Trilby, who brings a clearer harmony to the group, also unwittingly brings about its dissolution. This is foreshadowed in the narrator's mock lyric warning to all young men who think that their camaraderie is unending:

eighteen, nineteen, twenty, even twenty-five, who share each other's thoughts and purses, and wear each other's clothes, and swear each other's oaths, and smoke each other's pipes, and respect each other's lights o'love, and keep each other's secrets, and tell each other's jokes, and pawn each other's watches and merrymake together on the proceeds, and sit all night by each other's bedsides in sickness, and comfort each other in sorrow and disappointment with silent, manly sympathy—"Wait till you get to forty year! . . . Nay, wait till either or each of you gets himself a wife!" (147)

Little Billee begins to fall in love with Trilby and his strong feelings toward her gradually isolate him from Taffy and the Laird. His prudishness, especially with regard to sexuality, finally leads him to lose both Trilby and his prospects of happiness. One day he walks into an artist's studio and discovers Trilby posing in the nude. He was "so shocked and disgusted that he ran away" (123), Trilby reports. His actions have interesting consequences for Trilby. She had previously posed in the nude and never thought twice about it: "she was absolutely without that kind of shame, as she was without any kind of fear" (98). But after witnessing the revulsion of Little Billee toward her nudity, she feels shame for the first time and declares that she is "never going to sit again, not even for the face and hands." Little Billee has made her feel morally dirty: "Hitherto, for Trilby, self-respect had meant little more than the mere cleanliness of her body. . . . It now meant another kind of cleanliness" (127). Although she acknowledges that she has had lovers in the past her character comes across as that of a chaste, ingenuous girl. Her free and open spirit—like that of Murger's young women—is now, for the first time, fettered with shame. Later on, by refusing to accept Trilby as his mistress and demanding that they become married, he further complicates their relationship. After the intervention of Little Billee's mother and her clergyman brother-in-law, Trilby nobly runs off in order not to interfere with his prospects for success as a respectable, middle-class artist.

It is at this point in the story that the "happy times of . . . youth and hope and health and freedom—with all Paris for a playground" come to an end. The Laird asks Trilby, "what shall we do without you? . . . You've become one of us!" She replies that "it can't be any more now, can it? Everything is changed for me—the very sky seems different" (197). Little Billee is, of course, shattered by his loss and as the story leaps ahead five years we see a much changed Little Billee. Living now in London he has—as his mother hoped—become a wealthy, successful, and respected artist, with one of his paintings having appeared at the Royal Academy and now hanging in the National Gallery. But his emotional life has atrophied and he remains *Little* Billee in both stature and spirit: "It was as though some part of his brain where his affections were seated had been paralyzed, while all the rest of it was as keen and active as ever" (219). Like John Stuart Mill in the famous passage of his *Autobiography* in which he confesses his inability to feel emotion until he read the poetry of Keats, Little Billee has spent five years out of touch with his deepest feelings, and awaits their rebirth.

This theme of death and rebirth moves toward a climax when Little Billee first attends the performance of "La Svengali": "Little Billee had lost all control over himself, and was shaking with his suppressed sobs—Little Billee, who hadn't shed a single tear for five long years!" (320). The effect of seeing and hearing Trilby again resurrects Little Billee's lost youth and joy. Walking down a Parisian boulevard arm-in-arm with Taffy and the Laird, he allows his feelings to move outward to envelop the world, and he is reborn:

He wished to feel on each side of him the warm and genial contact of his two beloved old friends. It seems as if they had suddenly been restored to him, after five long years of separation, his heart was overflowing with affection for them, too full to speak just yet! Overflowing, indeed, with the love of love, the love of life, the love of death—the love of all that is, and ever was, and ever will be! just as in his old way.

. . . He was himself again at last, after five years, and wide awake; and he owed it all to Trilby! (335)

Little Billee's renewal and his sense of paradise regained prove to be short-lived. Svengali, who destroys Trilby, also destroys Little Billee, who must now face "the hideous pangs of jealousy so consuming that it would burn up his life" (337).

It is at this point that a concurrent theme of lost youth and innocence intersects with the one traced through Little Billee—that is, Svengali's corruption of Trilby. Early in the story we are told that Trilby had to face "one jarring figure in her little fool's paradise, a baleful and most ominous figure that constantly crossed her path, and came between her and the sun, and threw its shadow over her, and that was Svengali" (107). This paradise is sure to be ravaged and Svengali's various epithets, such as "black spider-cat," "incubus," "demon," "magician," and the fact that he draws his breath with a serpentlike hiss—all suggest that he is just the demon to do it. His sexual and psychic domination of her through mesmerism has already been explored. The results of his exploitation are exhibited in the rapid decline of Trilby once she is out of Svengali's control. Her beauty is described as "pathetic . . . so touching, so winning in its rapid decay" (414). She is suffering from a mysterious disease and her pallor and emaciation begin to accentuate the bones of her face. The decline also seems to indicate a loss of vital energy, just as vampire women die when Dracula is killed and they can no longer be sexual. It is as if she depended upon Svengali for her physical strength as she once did for her beautiful voice, and now that he is dead, she quickly loses her vitality, her youth, and even her memories:

she looked thirty at least—she was only twenty-three.

Her hands were almost transparent in their waxen whiteness; delicate little frosty wrinkles had gathered round her eyes; there were gray streaks in her hair; all strength and straightness and elasticity seemed to have gone out of her with the memory of her endless triumphs . . . and of her many wanderings from city to city all over Europe. (398)

By corrupting Trilby and using her like an exotic musical instrument, thereby reducing her to this morbid condition (foreshadowed in his earlier seductions), Svengali also destroys the only person who can restore to Little Billee his own lost romantic vision of a world built upon love, fellowship, and freedom. When Trilby dies, Little Billee dies soon after. Melodramatic, perhaps, but thematically sound. Trilby's brief time with Little Billee, the Laird, and Taffy was "her little fool's paradise," even as it was to Little Billee. The "black spider-cat" poisons and devours them both. Their romantic and youthful ideals rendered them the perfect victims.

The last chapter of the novel appropriately focuses upon Taffy. He is a survivor. Physically powerful, emotionally stable, and practical in worldly affairs, he marries a woman who fell in love with him twenty-five years earlier. Throughout the novel it was he who would stand up for Little Billee and tweak Svengali's nose and it was he who could comfort and advise Trilby in her difficulties. Unlike Little Billee and Trilby, he lived in the real world and was therefore immune to the poisonous sting of the demon-spider who played and preyed upon young dreamers.

An interesting side note to this theme is the way in which Du Maurier contrasts Paris and London. Paris is a playground for the "three musketeers of the brush." It is a city associated with youthful idealism, camaraderie, freedom, and joyful poverty. London is a city of lost dreams, lost youth, and lost fellowship. Several years after he returns to London, Little Billee becomes a respected, well-to-do, and joyless artist. His paintings hang in the famous London museums and are shown at the city's prestigious galleries. But all good things remain in the Paris of his dreams and memories. Interestingly, it is at Trilby's performance in Paris that Little Billee's love for Trilby is rekindled and he feels reborn. It is in London, however, that he witnesses her deterioration and death. The two cities take on symbolic values for innocence and experience, dream and reality, life and death, contrasts similar to the ones depicted in *Peter Ibbetson* between Passy and Pentonville.

The most pervasive image of life in Parisian chapters is that of food. With food comes good fellowship and good talk. More importantly, food seems to be a surrogate for sex. The hearty appetites of the "three musketeers of the brush" remind us of their flesh-and-blood reality:

the sting of healthy appetite was becoming intolerable; so they would betake themselves to an English eating-house in the Rue de la Madeline . . . , where they would renovate their strength and their patriotism on British beef and beer, and household bread, and bracing, biting, stinging yellow mustard, and horseradish, and noble apple-pie, and Cheshire cheese; and get through as much of these in an hour or so as they could for talking, talking, talking; such happy talk! (37)

There are many other meals described in mouthwatering detail, meals prepared by Taffy in their rooms, simple French meals in small, intimate restaurants—wine, beef, onions, garlic, butter, soups, herrings, cheese establish a very savoury atmosphere. The climax of the Parisian section comes with the Homeric feast in the studio on Christmas Day. Nearly twenty pages are devoted to a description of all the elaborate preparations for the meal, the invitation of their friends, the camaraderie during the feast, and the price of over indulgence to be paid the next morning. The meal itself includes plum pudding, mince pies, English sausages, Stilton cheese, sirloin of beef, "truffled galantines of turkey, tongues, hams, rillettes de Tours, pâtés de foie gras, saucissons d'Arles et de Lyon, with and without garlic, cold jellies peppery and salt," wine, English beers, chartreuse, curaçao, ratafia de cassis, and anisette. This incredible menu was based upon an actual dinner that Du Maurier enjoyed in 1856 at the lodgings of his artist friend Thomas Lamont. The feast in *Trilby* turns out to be a kind of Last Supper. The richness of life, here enjoyed in its most concentrated form, with its fine food and drink and good fellowship, is soon exchanged for disillusionment, quiet respectability, and emotional insensibility as Little Billee leaves Paris for London. The transition from an intense, sensual experience to one of depression suggests the pattern of a sexual experience. There is no mention of food in the more lifeless London chapters.

The emotional lives of Little Billee and Trilby begin to degenerate after they leave France:

Little Billee, with his quick, prehensile, aesthetic eye took many a long and wistful parting gaze at many a French thing he loved, from the gray towers of Notre Dame downward—Heaven only knew when he might see them again!—so he tried to get their aspect well by heart, that he might have the better store of beloved shape and color memories to chew the cud of when his lost powers of loving and remembering clearly should come back. . . . (213)

Five years later, when Little Billee returns to Paris and is reunited with Taffy and the Laird, who plan to hear "La Svengali," Du Maurier devotes an entire chapter to convey a sense of renewed life. Old acquaintances, buildings, streets, restaurants, and studios are revisited, and Paris becomes the city of light and promise it was years ago. When they return to their old art studio they find it very changed except for one essential—"Little Billee's old black-and-white-and-red chalk sketch of Trilby's left foot, as fresh as if it had been done only yesterday!" (302). The reunion with his friends and his walks through the city prepare Little Billee for his emotional reawakening during Trilby's great performance. A little later, in London, Svengali, Trilby, and Little Billee all die, and the reader is thereby melodramatically reminded of the "pathetic evanescence of things."

The Nostalgic Tone

Trilby is Du Maurier's only novel written from the omniscient point of view. By detaching himself from any one character, Du Maurier can better focus upon the two groups upon which the structure of the novel depends: Little Billee, Taffy, the Laird, and Trilby in part one; and Little Billee, Trilby, and Svengali in part two. The thematic movement from harmony to disharmony, from life to death is thus brought into sharp relief through the omniscient view point. The focus in *Peter Ibbetson* and *The Martian* is clearly upon their heroes, Peter Ibbetson and Barty Josselin, but here the focus is more diffuse as it shifts from Little Billee and his two seemingly inseparable friends, to Trilby, and to Svengali. The book's title suggests that Trilby is the main character, but the narrator spends more time examining the thoughts and feelings of Little Billee than of anyone else. In this sense, he comes closest to being the central figure in the story. The more dynamic and mysterious character of Svengali, however, overshadows all those around him. Still, since this is a novel about the decay of human relationships, and with these three contenders for its central focus, Du Maurier wisely decided upon a point of view that could more readily accommodate their claims upon his interest.

Despite the omniscient point of view Du Maurier expresses an ambiguous attitude toward his characters that reflects his ambivalence about sexuality and respectability. His real and sometimes deeply felt human prejudices are always apparent. He sympathizes and sometimes identifies himself with Little Billee; he admires Taffy and the Laird; he idealizes and adores Trilby; and he despises Svengali. Trilby is conceived in terms of superlatives: her's is "the handsomest foot in all Paris" and her voice becomes "not only faultless, but infallible." Sometimes his tone becomes discursive and defensive, as when he introduces a four-page digression on nudity. Facing a reading public that might fault Trilby for posing "in the altogether," Du Maurier argues that for the artist "nothing is so chaste as nudity." Svengali, on the other hand, is usually described in terms of loathing. He is physically dirty, he leers, he bullies, he hates. But despite the obvious repulsion that Du Maurier feels for him, he acknowledges his mastery of music: "He had been the best pianist of his time at the Conservatory at Leipsic" (58). The author's tone becomes more consistent and matter-of-fact, however, in setting forth the narrative line of the story.

Occasionally, as in his digression on nudity and his pronouncement on "impecunious, unpinnacled, young inseparables" that are fated to fall prey to marriage and conventional lives, the tone becomes didactic. The longest and most didactic digression is reserved for one of Du Maurier's favorite targets, religion. Instead of addressing the subject directly, Du Maurier has Little Billee indulge in a fourteen-page monologue (the only auditor being a patient dog named Tray), in which he proclaims his free thinking and extols the virtues of *Origin of*

Species. Although Du Maurier has similar passages in his other novels, he here disavows Little Billee's ideas: "I am not responsible for his ways of thinking (which are not necessarily my own)" (283). Granted that Little Billee's monologue is undermined by his youthful bravado and unscholarly mind, his sentiments nevertheless reflect the author's own.

The predominant tone of the novel, however, is one of nostalgia for youth, love, and beauty that are destroyed by time. It is a tone that reinforces one of the main themes of the novel discussed earlier. The fact that Svengali accelerates the destruction of youthful beauty accounts for the great evil that he represents and for Du Maurier's and his characters' fear and loathing of him. Henry James attempts to explain why and how Du Maurier's novels personally affect him in a distinctive, almost inexpressible manner, and suggests that their power lies in their elusive tone: "The whole performance is a string of moods and feelings, of contacts and sights and sounds. It is the voice of an individual, and individuals move to the voice, and the triumph is that they all together produce an impression, the impression that completely predominates, of the lovable, the sociable, of inordinate beauty and yet of inordinate reality."[10] The sense of beauty that will inevitably be lost and of youth that cannot endure bestows a quiet melancholy and pathos upon the tone of the entire novel and reinforces the theme that death is the mother of beauty. It is apparent even in the melodramatic death-bed scene where Little Billee, putting his ear to Trilby's mouth to hear her breathe, cries out: "Trilby! Trilby!" and Trilby, after uttering a brief sigh, speaks in a weak voice her last three words: "Svengali. . . . Svengali. . . . Svengali! . . ." (435). Her response comes as a surprise to anyone expecting a happy, sentimental conclusion in which she acknowledges her true feelings for Little Billee. But Trilby, the inordinate beauty, instead pays homage to the inordinate reality, Svengali, the force that has mastered her body and, perhaps, her soul. The nostalgic tone is most clearly heard in the description of Little Billee's complex feelings during Trilby's performance in Paris. He is overwhelmed by her beauty and song but then thinks of her lover: "And his old cosmic vision of the beauty and sadness of things, the very heart of them, and their pathetic evanescence, came back with a tenfold clearness—the heavenly glimpse beyond the veil" (324).

All of Du Maurier's novels reflect his bilingualism, but in *Trilby* he also experiments with various dialects that sharpen his characterizations. Trilby, for example, had an Irish father and a Scotch mother, and grew up in France, and now speaks "with an accent half Scotch" and with "certain French intonation." Trilby is not given a great deal of dialogue, but when she does speak it is either in French or a slightly modified English. When she first meets her three artist friends she exclaims, "Ye're all English, now, aren't ye?" But after it is established that Trilby is a unique creature, Du Maurier has her speak standard English or slangy French. He explains that "Trilby speaking English and Trilby speaking French were two different beings" (94). Her English is that of her highly educated father, but her French of the Latin Quarter stamped her as "emphatically 'no lady.'" Trilby's bilingualism anticipates the divisions later developed in the novel: between Paris and London, dream and reality, the natural Trilby and "La Svengali." This fundamental duality, reflected in the languages of his main characters, is a hallmark of Du Maurier's thinking about the world.

The French of Little Billee, Taffy, and the Laird is self-conscious and, in the case of the latter, Du Maurier describes it as "that English kind that breaks up the stiffness of even an English party" (46). The author has great fun with the Laird's awkward attempts at the language. In one scene he tries to imitate Trilby dancing the cancan, which he calls "le konkong," and every time he bows to acknowledge the applause that greeted his performance he said, "Voilà l'espayce de hom ker jer swee!" (105).

Svengali is given a peculiar dialect to suggest his foreign character. His background is shrouded in mystery. At one point he is designated a Polish Jew but later we are told that his parents and relatives are in Austria. He "spoke fluent French with a German accent, and humorous German twists and idioms" (12). His language is not always characterized by humor, however, for sometimes his "vicious imaginations . . . , which look so tame in English print, sounded much more ghastly in French, pronounced with a Hebrew-German accent"

(136). Since Du Maurier did not know German well, he has Svengali, on occasion, "speak in German," but gives us that speech in English. But Svengali's English, whether "translated" or spoken directly, is the same, an English marked by a German accent and by an occasional German word or phrase. He calls Trilby "Drilpy" and, upset when she is not listening to his prattle, he resorts to terms like "sapperment," "Dummkopf," and "Donnerwetter." But Du Maurier is careful to suggest rather than overwork the accent. He wants his speech to suggest the alien and grotesque nature of his villain, and too much fractured English would run the danger of making him a comic figure.

The comedy of accent is reserved for a character named Herr Kreutzer, a composer much impressed by Trilby's voice: "*All* music is koot ven *she* zings it. I forket ze zong; I can only sink of ze zinger. Any koot zinger can zing a peautiful zong and kif bleasure, I zubboce! But I voot zooner hear la Sfencali zing a scale zan anypotty else zing ze most peautiful zong in ze vorldt—efen vun of my own!" (259). The passage goes on at some length and the initial fun of the caricature quickly runs out. Du Maurier's German characters appear to be either villains or comic stereotypes.

The Characters

Du Maurier's ambivalent attitude about sexuality and Victorian morality is reflected in many of the characters of *Trilby*. Through the pivotal figure of Svengali he creates a powerful tale of sexual domination, with the character of Trilby as the focus of the erotic fantasy. An examination of the novel's characters will reveal Du Maurier's talent in developing this compelling fantasy, a talent that produced one of literature's great villains.

Trilby herself is a variation of the traditional Victorian heroine. She is full of life, charming, generous, humorous, naive, loving, and spontaneous. Modeled after Carry, the young girl whom Du Maurier and Moscheles met and tried to hypnotize in Malines, the character of Trilby is unlike the typical Victorian ingenue in one important respect: she has clearly lapsed from the all-important virtue of chastity. Du Maurier, however, defends his heroine's shortcoming:

But at least I am scholar enough to enter one little Latin plea on Trilby's behalf—the shortest, best, and most beautiful plea I can think of. It was once used in extenuation and condonation of the frailties of another poor weak woman, presumably beautiful, and a far worse offender than Trilby, but who, like Trilby, repented of her ways, and was most justly forgiven—"*Quia multum amavit!*"(53)

He also compares her to "a distinguished amateur who is too proud to sell his pictures, but willingly gives one away now and then to some highly valued and much admiring friend"(53). Like Thomas Hardy's Tess in *Tess of the D'Urbevilles*, Trilby is the familiar fallen woman with a heart of gold. Still, when she first appears in the novel her character is more like that of Haidee in Lord Byron's *Don Juan*. We are told that "Truly, she could be naked and unashamed—in this respect an absolute savage" (98). Like an unfallen Eve, her character radiates innocence and youthful vitality. She acquires a sense of guilt and sin only after Little Billee inflicts his English prudishness upon her. English respectability conquers French promiscuity in this clash of characters. In terms of the theme of the loss of innocence, it is ironic that Little Billee's conventional morality proves to be the serpent in Trilby's garden of paradise, an irony that reflects upon Du Maurier's choice of English respectability over French bohemianism for his own style of life.

Trilby's physical appearance also attests to her unorthodox character. In Du Maurier's other novels and in his drawings his ideal of female beauty consists of stature, elegance, and nobility, such as exhibited by the duchess of Towers. Trilby, however, has "thick, wavy brown hair, and a very healthy young face, which could scarcely be called quite beautiful at first sight, since the eyes were too wide apart, the mouth too large, the chin too massive, the complexion a mass of freckles" (15). Du Maurier's idealized women seem like statues but Trilby is very much a flesh-and-blood character whose strong physical presence reinforces her animal innocence. The fact that her feet are the most attractive parts of her body suggests how down-to-earth her beauty really is. "Seldom a thing of beauty in civilized adults," the foot, Du Maurier says, is usually "hidden away in disgrace, a thing to be thrust out of sight and forgotten" (19). But in the case of the "savage" Trilby, her feet were "astonishingly beautiful, such as one only sees in pictures and statues—a true inspiration of shape and color, all made up of delicate lengths and subtly modulated curves and noble straightnesses and happy little dimpled arrangements in innocent young pink and white" (18). Her feet become a fetish to the three young artists who admire, paint, and make plaster casts of them.

Whatever sexuality these Englishmen express seems openly directed at her feet. Little Billee's response to them is described as "a curious conscious thrill that was only half esthetic"(42). Trilby's animal innocence, her sexuality, and her beauty, then, are all symbolized by her naked feet. In Freudian psychology, the foot can be seen as a displacement for the pudendum. With the strict moral codes of the period, one's suppressed eroticism, when focused upon a part of the body most distant from the genitals, could be made socially acceptable and be enjoyed without guilt. *Webster's Third New International Dictionary* notes that the word "trilby," usually in the plural, became synonymous with feet, that after 1894 people began referring to their "trilbies."

How Du Maurier chose the name of his heroine is not totally clear. Some of the author's contemporaries traced the title of the novel to a story by Charles Nodier entitled *Trilby, or the Fay of Argyle*. Published in Paris in 1822, it tells the story of a fairy named Trilby who falls in love with a mortal woman named Jeannie. But outside of the title there is little resemblance between the two works. It may well be that Du Maurier first came upon the name from Nodier's rather obscure story, but another likely source, one that has never been noted, is Giuseppe Tartini's sonata for violin entitled *The Devil's Trill,* supposedly played to the composer by the devil in a dream. Given Du Maurier's wide knowledge of music and the fact that this is a famous and often performed piece, there is a likely connection with the novel. Furthermore, Tartini's title may have suggested the main theme of the novel: Trilby becomes the property and instrument of the demonic figure Svengali. She becomes the devil's Trilby as well as the devil's trill.

The name of the hero clearly is taken from Thackeray's ballad

"Little Billee," which Du Maurier heard sung at many after-dinner entertainments. The ballad tells the story of three friends who go off to sea, run out of food, and come close to cannibalizing the youngest member, Little Billee, because "he's young and tender." Some of Du Maurier's friends assumed that the character of Little Billee, because of his small stature, artistic talent, and early death, was based upon Frederick Walker, the illustrator and painter. Du Maurier, however, flatly denied the connection. It seems more likely that his character is drawn loosely after Du Maurier's own. Like his creator, Little Billee is small and slender, dark-haired, and has delicate, regular features. In an attempt to add an exotic quality to his hero, he notes that in his "handsome face there was just a faint suggestion of some possible very remote Jewish ancestor"(6). It may be that Du Maurier suspected that he himself had a strain of Jewish blood, for his other hero, Peter Ibbetson, has a distant Jewish ancestor on his mother's side, her first cousin being Colonel Ibbetson, the son of a Portuguese Jew. Little Billee is like Du Maurier in several respects: he admires and envies the aristocracy, he is a free thinker, he moves from a shallow though happy bohemianism in Paris to a successful middle-class life in London, he is a respected and respectable artist, he loves music, and he undergoes a nervous breakdown similar to Du Maurier's own in 1862.

Despite the autobiographical details, Little Billee is not a very sympathetic character. He is self-righteous, priggish, and frequently down-right dull. As we have already seen, it is his sense of moral superiority that drives Trilby away in shame. For much of the story he appears cold and unfeeling, and when he suffers his emotional breakdown he becomes even less appealing. His long monologue on religion is didactic and dull, and fails to communicate any real depth to his character. He becomes introspective, preoccupied with his own lack of feeling, and even though he is depicted as a successful artist he continues to be the same self-centered prig he was before. Lionized in London, he now "grew tired of the great before they had time to tire of him" (234). Bored with high society, "it was also his pleasure now and again to study London life at its lower end" (236) where he is said to have befriended many working men. But these occasional slumming trips to Whitechapel and the Minories merely emphasize Little Billee's self-indulgence and token humanitarianism. Nothing ever comes of these adventures or friendships.

After the memorable Christmas debauch, Little Billee experiences his first state of depression. Waking from a painful hangover, "it was as though a tarnishing breath had swept over the reminiscent mirror of his mind and left a little film behind it, so that no past thing he wished to see therein was reflected with quite the old pristine clearness" (182). This alcoholic haze nicely foreshadows the more significant blunting of Little Billee's sensibilities after he loses Trilby. As a solitary figure he remains consistently difficult to care about. What saves him at every turn are the vivacious and believable characters who support and surround him: Trilby, Taffy, and the Laird. In fact, what finally becomes apparent is that Little Billee is like a child who needs the constant attention afforded by his friends. The huge, powerful Taffy fights his battles for him. The Laird cooks for him. And Trilby sometimes seems to be more of a mother figure than a potential lover for Little Billee. After his drinking bout at the Christmas feast, he "had but one longing: that Trilby, dear Trilby, kind Trilby, would come and pillow his head on her beautiful white English bosom, and lay her soft, cool, tender hand on his aching brow, and then let him go to sleep, and sleeping, die!" (182). Alas, he does not die in such a Keatsian delirium, but rather in a state of jealousy. Having heard Trilby's dying words, her calling out to Svengali, Little Billee, on his own death-bed, agonizes over her past life with Svengali and the possibility that she will continue to be a slave to him in the afterlife. He dies like he lived, thinking about himself, his own loss, his own grief. Little Billee never really grows up to achieve a mature perspective on his relationship with Trilby and his friends. His narrow vision, self-righteousness, and ambition lead him to a misery that is punctuated with only a few brief moments of romantic joy. Neither his meddling mother nor Svengali is responsible for his despair, though he fails to recognize this to his dying day. Like an adolescent with uncompromising ideals, he prefers his dream vision over the reality of things and cannot accept the "beautiful white English bosom" of Trilby after it has cradled the head of the demon Svengali, with whom she will spend all eternity.

The character of Taffy is much more pleasant and comfortable. He appears to be a composite figure based upon the tall, powerful figure of Val Prinsep and the solid dependability of Thomas Armstrong. Taffy, "alias Talbot Wynne," is a Yorkshireman, but his name clearly suggests that he comes from a Welsh background. Not only is Wynne a well-known Welsh family name, but Taffy, his nickname, and a common Welsh Christian name, immediately calls to mind the famous ditty that begins "Taffy was a Welshman, Taffy was a thief." The name Taffy, in fact, has become a friendly slang term for a Welshman. Du Maurier does not comment directly on his name but the name itself would suggest to his readers the Welsh character—robust, generous, and down-to-earth. There is little of Merlin's magic in this character. His strength lies in his loyalty and in his muscles, and he is as strongly loyal to Britain as he is to his friends. He came out of the Crimean War without a scratch and he comes out of the novel with barely a bruise. He is the only character in the book who ends up happy and married. Both in life and in his paintings "Taffy was a realist" (10). He is a survivor, selfless as Little Billee was selfish. He uses his great strength sometimes just in playful exhibition but usually to protect his friends from harm. On more than one occasion he gives Svengali a good trouncing when he threatens Little Billee. His character may have been suggested by that of William Dobbin in *Vanity Fair*. Despite his dedicated loyalty to Little Billee, Taffy falls in love with Trilby and even proposes to her. Du Maurier never exploits this interesting subject of divided loyalties but instead, late in the story, simply has Taffy explain to Little Billee the fact that he loved her, proposed marriage, and was refused because she had begun to fancy Little Billee. So, in place of a psychological study in conflict, we simply get Little Billee's surprised reaction: "Taffy, what a regular downright old trump you are!" (342).

The character of Sandy McAllister, the Laird of Cockpen, is drawn after Du Maurier's friend, Thomas Lamont. Like the Laird, Lamont painted a series of undistinguished Spanish scenes, typified by a guitar-playing toreador serenading his lady. He is the least clearly drawn character of the trio and is easily confused with Taffy whom he resembles. He is important insofar as he rounds out the group, prepares hearty salads, and, in general, admires and helps to look after Little Billee.

A host of minor characters appears briefly in the course of the story and most of them are drawn after friends and relatives of the author. Du Maurier's brother Eugene and his friend Prince de Ligne appear as Dodor and l'Zouzou. These characters befriend Little Billee, who is at first embarrassed by their company: "As a respectably brought up young Briton of the higher middle class . . . it was not pleasant for him to be seen . . . walking arm in arm . . . with a couple of French private soldiers, and uncommonly rowdy ones at that" (150). Then there is Joe Sibley, "the idle apprentice," based upon Whistler, and his counterpart, Lorrimer, "the industrious apprentice," drawn after Edward Poynter. These characters are nicely contrasted in one illustration (later excised) entitled "The Two Apprentices." Sibley is in an affected pose, dressed like a dandy and holding a cane and a cigarette in an effeminate manner. Lorrimer, crossing behind him, and looking disapprovingly at him, is carrying all of his artist's paraphernalia as he heads briskly to work. Nevertheless, Du Maurier's description of Sibley—or Antony, as he came to be called—is rather generous: "for all of his reprehensible pranks, [he was] the gentlest and most lovable creature that ever lived in bohemia, or out of it . . . —the warmest, staunchest, sincerest, most unselfish friend in the world" (143).

Du Maurier apparently meant every word he said here about Whistler. Wild and reckless as he was, Whistler held a strong fascination for Du Maurier during those early days. He exhibited not only harmonious arrangements of light, form, and color in his paintings but a true bohemian spirit that Du Maurier greatly admired. Had he not been inhibited by his rigid English upbringing, Du Maurier would have readily adopted the exotic life style of his American friend. Lorrimer, on the other hand, is depicted in terms of both his life and art as a traditionalist, a serious, hard-working student of the Renaissance masters who finally achieves fame as an Academician. The portraits of both artists, sketchy though they may be, are reliable vignettes and appealed to Du Maurier's readers, who delighted in recognizing the real people behind the characters.

The masterful character of Svengali, however, is at the heart of the novel's success. Unlike all of the other figures in the book who are drawn after actual persons, Svengali emerges as a mythic character, one that transcends individual personalities and stands even today as an embodiment of a controlling evil genius. As a villain he is much more sinister and complex than Colonel Ibbetson. A tall, bony individual, Svengali is said to be between the age of thirty and forty-five, shabby, dirty, and dressed in old velveteen. Du Maurier maintains a careful air of mystery around him by not precisely defining his age (as he does with other characters), suggesting, perhaps, the agelessness of evil. He keeps his origins shrouded in mystery and even his present residence is unknown: "Nobody knew exactly how Svengali lived, and very few knew where (or why)." He is poor, a bully, possesses a cynical humor and "his laughter was always derisive and full of malice" (57). But despite his repulsive nature he is a musical genius. This, combined with his mysterious hypnotic powers, allows him to dominate his peers and eventually to control huge audiences in Paris and London. His faithful, doglike follower, Gecko, acknowledges his master's super powers: "Svengali was the greatest artist I ever met! Monsieur, Svengali was a demon, a magician! I used to think he was a god!" (452). "Demon," "magician," "god," "incubus," "black spider-cat"—these are the terms constantly associated with him and which suggest his mythic dimensions, the Orphic demon already discussed.

The question of why Du Maurier credits a Jew with supernatural powers is an interesting one. First of all, there is a convention of depicting the Jew as devil. In *Oliver Twist*, for example, Fagin is suggested to have Satanic powers, and Cruikshank's illustration of him bears a close resemblance to Du Maurier's drawing of Svengali. Edmund Wilson offers this further explanation:

What is really behind Svengali is the notion, again, that the Jew, even in his squalidest form, is a mouthpiece of our Judaico-Christian God, whose voice he has, in this case transferred ventriloquially, to the throat of Trilby. There is always in these novels of du Maurier's—binational, bilingual as he was—a certain light playing-off of French civilization against English; but the picture is further complicated—it is one of the things that make them interesting—by this dual role of the Jew, who appears—in Colonel Ibbetson, Svengali in his ordinary relations—now as a malignant devil, whose malignancy is hardly accounted for; now—in Leah, Little Billee and the Svengali who animates Trilby—as a spirit from an alien world who carries with it an uncanny prestige, who may speak in a divine tongue.[11]

Wilson's observation about the paradoxical, dual nature of Svengali is acute, and it is one that is supported by Du Maurier's own clearly ambiguous treatment of his villain. He is not, obviously, the black stage villain of Victorian melodrama, though he shares some of his superficial features, but a godlike demon who can control the behavior of human beings and sometimes, out of that control, create beauty—the angelic, heavenly voice of Trilby.

Edgar Rosenberg points out that Du Maurier significantly altered the legend of the Wandering Jew through his creation of Svengali: "The leading character of the legend . . . and the story in which he appeared remained unalterably humorless. Du Maurier changed all that. What he did was to combine certain elements of the traditional Aharuerus-magician type with elements of the stereotype of the Shylock tradition, and to make Svengali over into a grotesque."[12] In his wooing of Trilby, in his speech, in his appearance, and in his relationship to his underling apprentice, Gecko, Svengali is a comically grotesque figure. Du Maurier relates him to the legend of the Wandering Jew by describing "Svengali walking up and down the earth seeking whom he might cheat, betray, exploit, borrow money from, make brutal fun of, bully if he dared, cringe to if he must—man, woman, child, or dog—was about as bad as they make 'em" (59). As black magician, however, his character is treated more respectfully, as he expresses seductive and angelic song through the vocal cords of Trilby.

Five mythic figures, then, are embodied in the character of Svengali: the Wandering Jew, the prophet ("mouthpiece of our Judaico-Christian God," as Wilson phrases it), Orpheus, the Devil, and the incubus. Some of these archetypal figures, however, have been modified in some particulars. The Wandering Jew here can get his nose tweaked by Taffy and Orpheus is a demonic creature who uses his musical talents to acquire power and prestige. Comic, grotesque, terrifying, repulsive, oracular, restless, musical, demonic, and sexually oppressive, Svengali is a complex character that appeals to us on many levels at once.

Trilby on Stage

Shortly after *Trilby* was published an American playwright by the name of Paul Potter read the novel and was so fascinated by it that he wrote a stage version of the story which was produced by a Mr. A. M. Palmer's company at the Boston Museum in March, 1895. The production was so successful that several companies were immediately put on the road to play it throughout the country. Its first production in New York occurred at the Garden Theatre in April, and hundreds of people had to be turned away for lack of seating room. The great success of the play in America caught the attention of the English actor-manager, Beerbohm Tree, who requested the privilege of producing the play in England. A contract involving Tree, Du Maurier, and Potter was signed, and the play was produced at Manchester during the 1895 autumn tour of Tree's Company. Trilby was played by Dorothea Baird, a Shakesperian actress, and Svengali by Tree himself. It was usual in the actor-manager system for the actor-manager to produce the play and to get the best part for himself.

Although Baird was not a highly skilled or experienced actress, Du Maurier insisted that she play Trilby. After first seeing her he declared, "No acting will be wanted; for here *is* Trilby!"[13] Hoyar Miller, Du Maurier's son-in-law, saw the production and reports that Baird "was so natural and so simple, so entirely devoid of any stage artifice that one felt that had she been an actress of more experience half the charm and pathos of her performance would have been lost." But it was Tree's performance that captivated the audience. Here is Miller's account:

Tree's Svengali was the complete embodiment of the pictures and descriptions in the book: it was fantastic, weird and comical in turns, and rose to great heights of tragic intensity. His playing at the piano, his wild dancing at the studio supper-party, his delicious scene with the Rev. Thomas Bagot when he pulls down the model's skirt over her knee, and at last his failing strength, all combined to create a display of genius beyond all possible praise or commensuration. It was Tree's masterpiece of character-acting.[14]

The play's success in Manchester created a demand for first-night seats at the Haymarket Theatre in London, where it opened later in the month. The prince and princess of Wales occupied the Royal Box and although they applauded the performance the princess did not like Miss Baird having naked feet. A more serious critic of the play, however, was in attendance—George Bernard Shaw. He felt that the novel had been seriously compromised as a play: " 'Trilby' is the very thing for the English stage at present. No need to act or create character: nothing to do but make up after Mr. du Maurier's familiar and largely popular drawings, and be applauded before uttering a word as dear old Taffy, or the Laird, or darling Trilby, or horrid Svengali."[15] Shaw, unlike Miller, derives only cynical amusement from Tree's rendition of Svengali: "Imagine, above all, Svengali taken seriously at his own foolish valuation, blazed upon with lime-lights, spreading himself intolerably over the whole play with nothing fresh to add to the first five minutes of him." Bored with the stereotypes of Victorian melodrama, Shaw says that if he were Du Maurier he would "ask whether the theatre is really in such an abject condition that all daintiness and seriousness of thought and feeling must be struck out of a book, and replaced by vulgar nonsense before it can be accepted on the stage."[16]

Shaw's evaluation of Tree's Svengali, however, seems to be based upon a misreading of Svengali's character in the novel: "but surely even the public would just as soon—nay, rather—have the original Svengali, the luckless artist-cad (a very deplorable type of cad, whom Mr. du Maurier has hit off to the life), understanding neither good manners nor cleanliness, always presuming, and generally getting nose-pulled and bullied."[17] Shaw ignores the mythic qualities of the villain and sees him, simply, as a realistic artist-cad. Consequently, he attributes to Potter and Tree, rather than to Du Maurier, the creation of Svengali's sinister, archetypal traits: "why, then, should [Tree] absurdly decline into the stagey, the malignant, the diabolic, the Wandering-Jewish, and vainly endeavor to make our flesh creep?"[18] It may well be that Tree played the role too heavily in the grand, melodramatic style of the day, but Svengali is supposed to make our flesh creep. Miller's account of Tree attests to the fact that the comic and grotesque side of the villain was retained. Surely his diabolic and Wandering-Jewish character is equally important and certainly in keeping with his description in the novel. Shaw's observation about that description—"poor Svengali is *not* a villain, but only a poor egotistical wretch who provokes people to pull his nose"[19]—is clearly a misreading, one that trivializes his evil and ignores significant passages (and illustrations) in the novel.

Trilby-mania

The enormous popularity of both the book and the play led to what was called Trilby-mania. Parodies began to appear throughout the year 1895. In January Mary Kyle Dallas published *Biltry*, which burlesqued the style and plot of the novel and caricatured the illustrations.[20] This was succeeded by a poetic parody by Leopold Jordon entitled *Drilby Reversed*. In June Joseph Herbert and Charles Puerner produced a dramatic parody called *Thrilby*, in which the villain, Spaghetti, was adept at hypnotizing chairs and tables. On a more serious level, the Knoedler Gallery in New York featured Trilby paintings and other galleries won crowds by exhibiting photographs and prints from the book and play. In London the Fine Arts Society featured the original manuscript in a locked glass case.

The scene in the novel that was most thoroughly exploited for commercial purposes was the one in which Little Billee sketched Trilby's perfect foot on the wall of his apartment. Businessmen were obviously captitalizing on the foot fetishism and the sexual code of the foot. A New York caterer began featuring ice cream molded in the form of Trilby's foot. Then a manufacturer in Chicago made a lady's high-heeled shoe called "the Trilby," which sold for three dollars. Another firm in Philadelphia offered Trilby-style boots to the woman who could most closely match the dimensions of Trilby's foot. Even silver scarf pins shaped like Trilby's famous foot and "Trilby Sausage" were soon on the market.

During this time in both England and America newspapers and journals devoted sections of their publications to unearthing anything related to *Trilby*. Occasionally the readers' response was significant, as when one correspondent in the *Critic* identified Thackeray's ballad as the source for Little Billee's name. More often than not, however, eccentricity ruled the day. A Kansas City journalist, for example, claimed to have purchased Trilby's house in Paris, and put a plaque on the door to memorialize its former occupant. Like Sherlock Holmes, whose lodgings on Baker Street have moved out of fiction into reality, Trilby was becoming an actual person. Even some small areas in Florida were named after characters in the book: a town called Trilby, a lake called Little Billee, and a Svengali Square.

While the commercialization of the novel and the play was in full swing, the *Conservator* ("an exponent of the world movement in Ethics," published in Philadelphia by Walt Whitman's literary executor, Horace Traubel) published a curious pamphlet by Isaac Hull Platt entitled *The Ethics of Trilby*. Platt makes out an elaborate defense of the morality of the novel, an issue which he acknowledges with surprise has not been raised by the majority of readers. But he does quote an editorial in *Outlook* that charges Du Maurier with immorality, for "in life innocence is not retained after virtue is lost." He begins his defense by referring to the story of Mary Magdalen and declares that "if 'Trilby' is immoral, the gospel attributed to St. John is immoral." But his most interesting observation concerns the double standards in nineteeth-century sexuality: "Reverse the case in regard to sex. Would any one allege that a story in which a man who had been guilty of unchastity in early life should be depicted as brave, generous, humane, self-sacrificing, is immoral?" Platt, finally, looks toward the day when "a fallen woman may be given a chance to redeem herself, and yet the life and purity of our American homes survive."[21]

It seems, then, that everyone from businessmen to liberal theologians, not to mention the hundreds of thousands of readers and playgoers, profited from Du Maurier's story in one way or another. But after the author died in 1896 the *Trilby*-mania began to subside, and by 1900 both the novel and the play were overshadowed by the works of authors like H. G. Wells, Thomas Hardy, and Oscar Wilde. But the powerful impression made by the mysterious Polish Jew, Svengali, survives. Several film versions were made in Hollywood, the first full-length one being Richard Walton Tully's silent film entitled *Svengali*, in 1922. Tully sought out for his location shots all of the places in Paris mentioned in the book. In 1931, after talking-pictures came into being, Tully produced a talking version of his film, again entitled *Svengali* and got John Barrymore to play the leading role. A more recent production was an English film of the same title directed by Noel Langley in 1954. Finally, in 1982, a made-for-television movie updated the story by making the character of Trilby, played by Jodie Foster, a rock music star. Even for those who have never read the book or seen the play or motion pictures, the name of Svengali has become synonymous for anyone who exercises a sinister control over another person.

Chapter Five
The Martian
Autobiographical Fantasy

Trilby brought fame, wealth, and prestige to Du Maurier, but he much regretted the erosion of his privacy. Nevertheless, he was now an international figure and the public was waiting to see what he would do next. He wrote to John Millais in 1894 that he was trying hard to conceive another book: "Sometimes I think it will come; sometimes I feel like giving it up and writing my reminiscences, which are very mild compared with yours."[1] By December of that year he had begun the actual writing, a task that proved very difficult for him. Lacking the inspired fluency that characterized his composition of the first chapters of *Peter Ibbetson*, he had now become a meticulously self-conscious author: "I revise, very carefully now, for I am taking great pains with my new book."[2]

Du Maurier's comment to Millais is significant because it reveals the author's autobiographical passion, one that was not to be denied in this, his last, novel. *The Martian* turned out to be the most autobiographical of all Du Maurier's works. Although he revised the manuscript at every stage and created a thorough and largely accurate account of his life, the book is sadly lacking the genuine enthusiasm for life and the lyricism that characterized his earlier novels. Perhaps because he put so much of himself into this work, he considered it his favorite and best book. He completed it in July, only a few months before his death in October, 1896. Later that month *The Martian* began to appear in *Harper's Monthly Magazine*, where it ran until July, 1897. Du Maurier had planned to follow this work with another fantastic novel, about an ordinary middle-aged and middle-class couple who discover that they can fly and who visit exotic lands throughout the world. Perhaps it is a blessing that he never began this project, for it sounds like an awkward and literal working out of the mòre interesting travels of Peter Ibbetson and the duchess of Towers who could move through time as well as space.

The hero of *The Martian* is Barty Josselin, the son of an English lord and a beautiful French actress of the lower class. Ormond notes that Jocelyn was a Du Maurier family name (it was one of Ellen Clarke's names) and that Du Maurier connected it with the great Rohan family, who lived at Castle Josselin in Brittany. Barty's grandfather, the Marquis of Whitby, lives at Castle Rohan, and has the crest of the actual Rohan family: "I am the king; I do not condescend to be prince; I am a Rohan." Barty combines the best characteristics of both lineages: he is an exceptional athlete, physically powerful, and yet remarkably handsome, tall, and refined.

The narrator of the story is Bob Maurice, Barty's closest friend, who presents in the first part of the book a straightforward account of Josselin's life. During this section Maurice is present at most of the scenes he describes. They are both students at the Pension Brossard, arriving there in 1847, the same year Du Maurier entered the Pension. Froussard. Du Maurier remarked to his friend Robert Sherard that "I shall write my school life in my novel 'The Martian.'"[3] According to his biographer, the experiences of Barty and Maurice at school exactly parallel those of Du Maurier and his brother Eugene. The undistinguished student life that Maurice led reflects Du Maurier's own experience at school, but it is Josselin, ironically, who fails the baccalaureate. It is at this point that Du Maurier splits his autobiography between his two characters. After they leave school, Maurice returns to London where, like his creator, he attempts to become a scientist. He enters University College in 1851 and two years later his father arranges for him to have his own laboratory. He subsequently enters his family business and eventually rises to become a member of Parliament and a baronet.

Maurice's uneventful and dreary life is contrasted with the glamorous and romantic career of his friend, Barty, an incredible hero who radiates an improbable number of virtues. Well over six feet tall, this paradigm of charm and grace enters the guards and becomes one of the most sought-after young men in London. Beautiful and aristocratic ladies vie with one another for his attention, and he manages to come through several love affairs without once losing his finesse or respectability. One recalls that Du Maurier's own young life in London, by contrast, was terribly lonely and that he made pathetic boasts to his mother that he was the center of attention among the social elite. Barty's life parallels Du Maurier's as he leaves art school in Paris, goes to Antwerp, loses the sight in one eye, and goes through a period of depression and anxiety.

As a child Barty possessed a "sense of the North." Even when blindfolded he could point to the north. This mysterious mental ability is a foreshadowing of his subsequent communication with Martia, a creature from Mars who speaks to Josselin in his sleep. She first appears in the novel after Josselin loses sight in one eye and is about to poison himself. A knock at the door momentarily distracts him and when he returns to his room the cyanide has disappeared. He discovers in its place a letter in his own coded handwriting, called Blaze, apparently dictated to him by Martia. She comforts him by explaining that the damage to the one eye will not affect his good eye and that she will continue to strengthen and support him: "If I were to let you destroy your body, as you were so bent on doing, the strongest interest I have on earth would cease to exist."[4]

Thus, midway through the novel, the autobiographical details suddenly give way to fantasy. This is the same arrangement that Du Maurier employed in *Peter Ibbetson* and *Trilby*. In all three novels the fantasy is rooted in Du Maurier's psyche. It is just possible that Peter Ibbetson, for example, as a madman only dreams he is "dreaming true," and Du Maurier makes it very clear that Martia may be only a figment of Barty Josselin's imagination, a figure conjured up amid a state of profound depression. He never states that she actually exists. And even Svengali's mental powers are given credibility by contemporary science. Thus the sudden appearance of Martia halfway into the novel, surprising and farfetched as it seems, nevertheless has some psychological cogency. The autobiography continues throughout the novel, but now in a more disguised form.

Martia's letter to Barty lifts his spirits and he moves from Antwerp to Dusseldorf and then on to London, where he begins work as an illustrator. He marries a dark-haired, penniless girl named Leah Gibson, whom he had known when he was in the Guards. She possesses an exotic Jewish beauty, like Sir Walter Scott's Rebecca, and is an idealization of Du Maurier's wife, Emma Wightwick. They are married in Marylebone Church where the Du Mauriers were wed, and their first daughter is born on the same day as Beatrix Du Maurier.

Martia's next visitation is to set up a program for Barty's future success. She will function as a sort of daemon or muse, who will use his knowledge and his words to fashion immortal works of literature. She gives him a reading list so that he can cultivate a decent English style: "I can only use your own words," she writes, "and your way of using them." She also permits him to inform Leah about her existence: "she'll think you've gone mad: but she'll have to believe you in time" (350). And thus begins the menage à trois, certainly one of the most bizzare in literary history.

Martia continues to visit Barty in his sleep and feeds him ideas that he records and embellishes during the day. Before long he is the author of several best-selling books, including *Sardonyx*, *The Fourth Dimension*, *Motes in a Moonbeam*, *Interstellar Harmonics*, *Bertha with the Large Feet*, *Dead Stars*, *The Footprints of Aurora*, and *The Infinitely Little*, to name a few. Maurice informs us that these novels "have had as wide and far-reaching an influence on modern thought as the *Origin of Species*" (358). Neither the theses of these books nor the nature of their powerful influence is ever explained, and the whole business of Barty's literary success is stated simply as a fact. Maurice's wild admiration for these absurdly titled books that no one has ever heard of and his refusal to discuss them and their great ideas make him seem a true hero-worshipper.

Having won international fame for Barty, Martia explains more fully her previous life on Mars. Over a great period of time she has undergone countless reincarnations, from the lowest form to the highest. She has forgotten all but her present form, which is comparable to that of a woman on earth. She goes on at great length to describe details of Martian life, its language, magnetism, terrain, and social customs. Martia came to earth a hundred years ago in a shower of shooting stars and fell in love with the beauty of the new planet. Now, as a disembodied spirit, she seeks another reincarnation, one more fulfilling than the occasional dwelling within Barty Josselin. She thus makes the startling announcement to Barty that she will be his next child: "Barty, when I am a splendid son of yours or a sweet and lovely daughter, all remembrance of what I was before will have been wiped out of me until I die. But *you* will remember, and so will Leah, and both will love me with such a love as no earthly parents have ever felt for any child of theirs yet" (402). At the conclusion of her long farewell letter, Maurice simply notes, "So much for Martia—whoever or whatever it was that went by that name in Barty's consciousness," an observation that reinforces the psychological theme. As will be shown later, Martia becomes more than a simple voice in Barty's mind. She represents Du Maurier's ambivalent attitude toward his mother.

In any event, the Josselins' seventh daughter and ninth child is born and named Martia, or Marty for short. She grows up to be a model child, bright, imaginative, refined, and very beautiful. One day she is climbing a tree, falls, and injures her spine. She never really recovers from the injury and it leads to an illness that lasts four years, a period during which the family is brought closely together. Barely a young woman, Marty finally dies, calling out "Barty—Leah—come to me, come!" (457). Barty Josselin dies at this same moment and Leah alone remains: "She's a noble woman; she seems to bear it well," the doctor tells Maurice.

Science and Pseudo-Science

There are not many precedents for the strange story that Du Maurier created in *The Martian*. It does contain a vague resemblance to several supernatural stories by Bulwer Lytton. The theme of reincarnation and the elaborate discourses on metaphysics and science can be found in *A Strange Story*. Barty's messages from the disembodied Martia resemble the hero's ability in *Zanoni* to communicate with a beautiful, ethereal intelligence named Adon-ai, a talent which he loses after he falls in love. Martia's description of life on Mars is similar to that of the subterranean inhabitants in the utopian novel, *The Coming Race*. And like Bulwer Lytton, Du Maurier uses the technique of employing familiar and specific details to establish a believable context for the supernatural occurrences.

Du Maurier believed that he had valid scientific grounds for his conception of life on Mars. In 1867 he read Sir David Brewster's book, *More Worlds Than One*, and was intrigued by the physicist's theories about life on other planets. Here is the passage that inspired Du Maurier's description of the intelligent, animal-like Martians:

To assume that the inhabitants of the planets must necessarily be either men or anything resembling them, is to have a low opinion of that infinite skill which has produced such a variety in the form and structure and functions of vegetable and animal life. . . . On a planet more magnificent than ours, may there not be a type of reason of which the intellect of Newton is the lowest degree? . . . The being of another mould may have his home in subterranean cities warmed by central fires,—or in crystal caves cooled by ocean tides,—or he may float with the Nereids upon the deep.[5]

In Du Maurier's depiction, the Martian "is amphibious, and decends from no monkey, but from a small animal that seems to be something between our seal and our sea-lion" (365). His senses are extremely acute and he possesses a sixth sense of the magnetic current, which is stronger in Mars than on earth. Thus Barty's "sense of the North." Martians evolve through a series of reincarnations from the lowest form to the highest, the final state being one of mental, moral, and physical superiority to the human condition. Yet, their lives are simple, communal, and they feed exclusively upon edible moss, roots, and submarine seaweed. They are great engineers, and sculpt beautiful underwater caves in which they live. Their race "is still developing towards perfection with constant strain and effort, although the planet is far advanced in its decadence and within measurable distance of its unfitness for life of any kind" (368).

Du Maurier's thesis of moral, physical, and mental evolution tending toward perfection owes something to Charles Darwin's conclusion to *Origin of Species*:

Thus, from the war of nature, from famine and death, the most exalted object which we are capable of conceiving, namely, the production of the higher animals, directly follows. There is grandeur in this view of life, with its several powers, having been originally breathed by the Creator into a few forms or into one; and that, whilst this planet has gone cycling on according to the fixed law of gravity, from so simple a beginning endless forms most beautiful and most wonderful have been evolved.[6]

There were a whole host of popularizers who helped to arouse interest in the subject of evolution and to give the reader the necessary elementary knowledge to understand it. These authors include Robert Chambers (*Vestiges of the Natural History of Creation*, 1844), Hugh Miller (*The Testimony of the Rocks*, 1857), Philip Henry Gosse (*The Romance of Natural History*, 1860), and George Henry Lewes (*Studies in Animal Life*, 1862). Chambers, for example, urges the idea that man himself is still evolving and will one day develop into a higher form. The laureate himself, Alfred Lord Tennyson, reflects the idea of Chambers throughout his great elegy, *In Memoriam*: "A soul shall draw from out the vast / And strike his being into bounds, / And, moved thro' life of lower phase, / Result in man, be born and think, / And act and love, a closer link / Betwixt us and the crowning race / Of those that, eye to eye, shall look / On knowledge."[7] He asserts his belief not only in human development but in the progress of the entire race, and he looks to the time when man will have evolved into a species "no longer half-akin to brute."

Martia asserts the same thesis, "that the race is still developing towards perfection with constant strain and effort," and because of this evolutionary drive she seeks another reincarnation, this time as the child of Barty and Leah. The theme is archetypal: a god or superior being is born of a mere mortal, or, in some cases, a god impregnates a mortal. In her annunciation Martia tells Barty, "It's a good seed that we have sown, you and I. It was not right that this beautiful planet should go much longer drifting through space without a single hope that is not an illusion, without a single hint of what life should really be, without a goal" (405). The goal and hope is the perfection of the race through eugenics. Martia explains that a speck at the back of Barty's brain contains a seed that will develop through his offspring: "If they pair well, and it is in them to do so if they follow their inherited instinct, their children and their children's children will have that speck still bigger." "When that speck becomes as big as a millet-seed in your remote posterity," Martia continues, "then it will be as big as in a Martian, and the earth will be a very different place, and man of earth greater and even better than the Martian by all the greatness of his ampler, subtler, and complex brain." Thousands of years in the future this speck will grow to the size of an orange and "the seed of Barty and Leah will overflow to the uttermost ends of the earth, and finally blossom and bear fruit for ever and ever beyond the stars" (406). There is some confusion about whose seed is sown. Earlier Martia says "It's a good seed we have sown, you and I," and now she speaks of it as "the seed of Barty and Leah." Despite the mystical biology, this view of racial evolution clearly echoes Tennyson's lines from *In Memoriam* that celebrates the "one far-off divine event / To which the whole creation moves." Both Du Maurier and the laureate thus postulate a teleological universe, one that will bring about the perfection of the human race.

The movement toward moral and spiritual perfection in *The Martian* is accomplished through a series of rebirths. Du Maurier fuses the ancient belief in reincarnation with the new doctrine of evolution as the basis of Martia's philosophy. Du Maurier was not an intellectual and his characters' quasi-scientific, quasi-religious discourses are shallow and confused. Martia has already evolved through a series of reincarnations to the highest form known among Martians. This form is one that is superior to the human, and when she is reborn as Barty's and Leah's daughter she in no way demonstrates that she has progressed toward a higher form. Rather, she appears to have taken a large step backwards, as she grows up to be a rather ordinary Victorian young lady whose frailty soon leads her to four years in a sickbed and an early death. And so, the whole notion of a superior being from another planet coming to earth to be reincarnated into a higher form is trivialized by the conclusion. A brilliant, disembodied intelligence is reborn as a girl who loved "fun and frolic and pretty tunes" and who, at age seventeen, dies of influenza. The spirit of Martia was much more effective when working through Barty's mind, for at least then she was able to produce through him a series of influential novels. All in all, however, Du Maurier's philosophy and fiction are clumsily intertwined to create a farcical and melodramatic conclusion.

Besides the contemporary interest in life on another planet, evolution, and reincarnation, the novel incorporates the subject of automatic writing. By the middle of the nineteenth century, especially after the development of hypnosis, the practice of automatic writing was studied by the Society for Psychical Research and soon became a widespread phenomenon. It was believed that a person in a state of sleep or, especially, in a hypnotic trance could receive messages from the dead. The entranced person, inhabited by a second personality, would write these messages down, sometimes in the style of the deceased. The Society reported in its journal numerous cases of automatic writing during the 1880s and 1890s, and the subject was popularized for the reading public, though not to the same degree as the practice of hypnotism.

The extra twist that Du Maurier gives to the subject is having a creature from another planet be the one to write through her medium. It is never made very clear to what extent Barty's novels are really his own. He literally writes them, first in his coded style called Blaze, and then in standard English or French, but one is led to believe that Martia provided him with all the ideas. Here is what we learn about the process from Martia's directions to Barty: "I will never trouble your rest for more than an hour or so each night. . . . You will have to work during the day from the pencil notes in Blaze you will have written during the night, and . . . anytime you are conscious of my presence, read what you have written during the day, and leave it by your bedside when you go to bed, that I may make you correct and alter and suggest—during your sleep" (351).

The Theme of Duality

What saves all of the supernatural paraphernalia from destroying the credibility of the novel is the narrator's important assertion that Barty "might, in short, have led a kind of dual life, and Martia might be a simple fancy or invention of his brain in an abnormal state during slumber" (352). Here is a thesis with considerable psychological plausibility, the same one that determined the structure of *Peter Ibbetson*. The great difference here is that Barty's dual life is perceived much more indirectly, through the elaborate reporting of his narrator-friend Bob Maurice. Peter Ibbetson narrates his own story from a madhouse and leaves the reader to decide upon his sanity. Maurice, on the other hand, is a sane, reliable narrator who, for all his hero worshipping of Barty, still records a modicum of doubt about the reality of Martia. The reader, therefore, need only believe that Barty believes in his extraterrestrial, nocturnal visitor. Du Maurier's audience might have been able to accept more readily than a twentieth-century reader the accounts of life on Mars, the doctrine of reincarnation and spiritual evolution, and the practice of automatic writing. The modern reader clutches anxiously to Maurice's passing skepticism in order to find some basis upon which to build his credibility in the plot. Du Maurier does not elaborate upon the possibility that Barty is self-deluded or is the master of wish-fulfillment, but he certainly leaves room for the reader to accept Martia as a psychological oddity.

Barty's relationship with Martia and his wife is an intriguing and complex one that perhaps reveals Du Maurier's ambivalent feelings about his mother. Martia is a sort of idealized mistress who visits her lover by night, in his sleep, and shares and directs his deepest thoughts. She first appears in order to save his life and to comfort him, after which she declares her spiritual love for him: "I love you Barty, with a love passing the love of woman; and have done so from the day you were born." Sometimes her feelings suggest that she is more than a spirit, as when she exclaims, "especially I love your splendid body and all that belongs to it—brain, stomach, heart, and the rest; even your poor remaining eye, which is worth all the eyes of Argus." She shares his senses and is physically one with Barty in the intimacy of sleep: "Whenever the north is in you, there am I; seeing, hearing, smelling, tasting, feeling with your five splendid wits by day—sleeping your lovely sleep at night" (255). Her invisibility makes her the near perfect mistress and she demaands that Barty not mention her to any living soul.

Toward the middle of the novel Martia reappears to urge Barty to marry the wealthy Julia Royce. Martia now becomes a mother figure instead of a mistress and sounds remarkably like Ellen Clarke, Du Maurier's society-conscious mother, who was unhappy with her son's interest in Emma and strongly urged him to marry an heiress. Martia pleads with Barty to marry Julia because she is "one of the richest girls in England, one of the healthiest and most beautiful women in the whole world, a bride fit for an emperor." The pathway to success is through an aristocratic connection (and a mother's wise advice): "It is in you to become so great when you are ripe that she will worship the ground you walk upon; but you can only become as great as that through her and through me, who have a message to deliver to mankind here on earth." Martia's last comment in this maternal lecture focuses upon Barty's social and physical defects: "Poor as you are, maimed as you are, irregularly born as you are, it is better for her that she be your wife than the wife of any man living, whoever he be" (293).

Like Barty, Du Maurier did not heed his mother's advice: "Who was Martia? What was she? 'A disembodied conscience?' Whose? Not his own, which counselled the opposite course" (295). Barty rejects the blonde, aristocratic Julia Royce for the poor, dark-haired Jew, Leah Gibson, even as Du Maurier, in his Dusseldorf days, had chosen the dark-haired Emma Wightwick over the affluent Louisa Lewis. As the voice of conscience, Martia greatly disturbs Barty's peace of mind, and he questions her identity in a way that reveals part of her complexity: "tell me, for God's sake, who you are and what! Are you *me*? Are you the spirit of my mother? Why do you love me . . . with a love passing the love of woman? What am I to you? Why are you so bent on worldly things?" (300). Martia never really answers these questions, but she is everything Barty surmises, and more. She is Barty himself in the sense that she is a voice in his mind, and she is also the voice of his mother, sometimes snobbish and other times comforting. Finally, she resembles the legendary succubus—a female demon supposed to descend upon and have sexual intercourse with a man while he sleeps—though in concession to Victorian morals, she appears to be chaste.

After Barty has married "among the daughters of Heth," and he and Leah have their first child, Martia, after nearly a year of silence, again communicates with her host to let him know that she now finds Leah to be an acceptable wife for him. She urges him to tell Leah all about her, as soon as Leah recovers from childbirth. It is at this point that she sets forth her plan to make Barty a famous writer: "Keep this from everybody but Leah; don't even mention it to Maurice until I give you leave" (351). As Martia continues to set up an intellectual

and literary household in Barty's brain, Leah develops into the perfect
Victorian wife: "full of sympathy . . . absolutely sincere, of a constant and even temper, and a cheerfulness that never failed . . . generous, open-handed, . . . of unwearied devotion to her husband, and
capable of any heroism or self-sacrifice for his sake . . ." (353). While
she is making the family household a model of domestic peace and
congeniality, Barty is busily writing novel after novel under the
nocturnal influence of Martia. Leah now takes on the roles of wife and
mother to the successful Barty: "She was really a mother to him, as
well as a passionately loving and devoted helpmeet" (362). It is never
clear when or how he related the story of Martia to his wife. Maurice
simply reports that he did so but "even now I hardly know what to
think, nor did Leah—nor did Barty himself up to the day of his death"
(362).

Leah's Jewishness has elicited some curious commentary. One
critic believes that Du Maurier represents her as a paragon of womanhood, suited to be the mother of the "choosy Martia," and an "official
symbol of apology for the presentation of Svengali."[8] There is no
evidence that Du Maurier ever felt that such an apology was necessary.
As already discussed in an earlier chapter, Du Maurier's attitude
toward Svengali was complex and combined conflicting emotions of
fascination and disgust. Leah, on the other hand, is a Jew, and as such
she is the embodiment of the archetypal mother—the Beautiful
Virgin, the Mother of God. It is this association that Du Maurier is
drawing upon for the mother of the goddess Martia.

Not only is she not a "symbol of apology," she is a transfigured
Jew, as the critic above observes: "Had Du Maurier not explicitly
affixed the label 'Jewess' (or its French equivalent), she would remain
indistinguishable from the rest of his lovely giantesses."[9] Du Maurier
depicts the Virgin Jew in terms of literary romance suitable to the
wife of his beautiful man:

It [the Sephardic Jew] is a type that sometimes, just now and again, can be
so pathetically noble and beautiful in a woman, so suggestive of chastity and
the most passionate love combined—love conjugal and filial and maternal—
love that implies all the big practical obligations and responsibilities of
human life, that the mere term "Jewess" (and especially its French equiva-

lent) brings to my mind some vague, mysterious, exotically poetic image of all I love best in woman. I find myself dreaming of Rebecca of York, as I used to dream of her in the English class at Brossard's, where I so pitied poor Ivanhoe for his misplaced constancy. (140)

Leah is a composite of several figures, including Du Maurier's own wife. She is the Jewish Virgin who gives birth to a goddess. She is the new Eve from whose children will evolve a physically and morally superior race. She is also the exotic heroine of romance. And as a tall, stately beauty, that blends into one with the duchess of Towers, Madame Seraskier, and the countless elegant women Du Maurier drew for *Punch*, Leah does indeed epitomize the author's ideal: "the poetic image of all I love best in women." Included in this ideal, of course, is the devotion of a typical Victorian wife, solicitous of her husband's every wish, devoted to their children, and scrupulous in fulfilling her domestic duties. She is the sort of idealized housewife and helpmate depicted in Coventry Patmore's poem, significantly entitled *The Angel in the House*.

Throughout his married life, then, Barty leads a dual existence and as far as the reader knows neither Martia nor Leah is jealous of the other. Martia could be viewed as the Muse-mistress of the novelist and Leah, as the perfect wife, simply accepts her husband's total dedication to his mistress, art. Indeed, Emma Du Maurier was very much like Leah in her unselfish support of her husband's career both before and after he won fame and riches with *Trilby*. But Martia is more than simply Barty's muse.

For one thing, Martia is not an emblem of Platonic or Christian love. She is too concerned about the physical body of the hero for that. Furthermore, she is an admirer of "worldly success, rank, social distinction, the perishable beauty of outward form, the lust of the flesh and the pride of the eye" (371). She is, however, straitlaced and was offended by Barty's loose behavior during his life as a Guardsman. The subject of sex is, not surprisingly, never opened with reference to either Martia or Leah. After Barty sows his wild oats as a Guardsman, there are no direct sexual references made during the rest of the novel. Du Maurier, like his literary hero, William Makepeace Thackeray, took great pains to keep the sex lives of his characters well within the bounds of Victorian propriety. Nevertheless, Martia's nocturnal visits are suggestive of the legendary succubus. Barty's mysterious lover is at first kept secret, her story only revealed after he achieves respectability through his inspired stories. Martia loves Barty, fertilizes his imagination, and makes him productive. She takes on the traditional masculine role of the aggressor in their relationship, while he passively and willingly accepts her dominance.

The fruits of their mental marriage consist at first of the novels, but Martia is not satisfied with such symbolic progeny and insists upon becoming the actual child of Barty and Leah: "my desire for reincarnation has become an imperious passion not to be resisted." Since Leah appears not to believe in Martia, thinking her a "somnambulistic invention" of her husband's mind, Martia's fantastic assertion that "I am going to be your next child" (400), does not apparently create any disunity in the Josselin household. The biology of such a pregnancy is, of course, never explained, and one must accept the birth of Marty as a sort of mystical enterprise—or, again, an ordinary event that Barty's fertile imagination converts into a supernatural occasion.

The psychological implications of all this are intriguing. Beneath the complex web of relationships there appears to be a fundamental Oedipal conflict. A mother-mistress figure, through a strange, mystical intercourse, becomes the daughter of a son-lover figure. This is not the first time that Du Maurier has fused the character of a daughter and mother. Madame Seraskier and the duchess of Towers become as one in the mind and emotions of Peter Ibbetson. The duchess of Towers, like Martia, also enjoined the roles of mother and dream-lover in her relationship with Peter. And, one might argue, when Peter returned in his dreams to his youth, he could enjoy watching the young Mimsey as if she were his daughter. Both Mimsey and Marty are innocents, frail in health, lovers of music and literature. They are like twin sisters in looks and character.

Leah, for all her exotic beauty, is relegated to the role of a minor character toward the last part of the novel where Martia clearly becomes Barty's chief concern. It is not clear how much Leah actually knows or believes about Martia. She simply bears the child and serves as an attentive, loving mother to Barty's most significant creation.

After the birth of Marty there is no mention of Barty's writing other novels. Martia can no longer inspire him now that she has been reincarnated as his daughter. But if the geni has been let out of the bottle, so to speak, in her new and freer form as Marty she continues to stimulate his literary productions. In the background Leah continues to administer the domestic details while Barty devotes all of his attention to Marty, his books, and his drawings. The climax of Barty's long involvement with Martia comes with the simultaneous death of Barty and Marty. First Martia shared his mind and body, then became his child, and now, in death, they are reunited as one spirit. Leah briefly survives in the mundane world she has always inhabited, an outsider, who never shared her husband's more rarified level of existence. The curious trinity of Barty-Martia-Marty is self-contained and self-referring. The union between Barty and Martia gives rise to Marty, a spiritual conception. Poor Leah is a sort of incubator, a midwife to a dream come true. With Marty's death, the triangle collapses upon itself. Barty is now totally possessed by his demon and Leah, with her nobility, "seems to bear it well." She must not have borne her grief too well, however, for earlier in the novel Maurice reported that she lived only twenty-four hours after her husband's death. Since her husband was her "fixed star" and she shone "with no other light than his," she apparently no longer had any reason to live without him. Such a melodramatic death clearly exhibits the male fantasy that a woman has no real life of her own and can live only through her husband.

The Beautiful Man

One cannot comfortably read this novel, like *Peter Ibbetson*, as the story of a madman. Although both novels have as heroes men who move between actual and dream worlds, in *The Martian* Du Maurier creates his most complete fantasy character, one who fulfills most of the author's wishes. The narrator, Bob Maurice, expresses a continual and uncritical admiration of the hero. Barty Josselin is physically perfect, possesses such an array of talents that all sorts of accomplishments come easy to him, and everyone he meets succumbs to his charm. At the very opening of the novel, Bob Maurice enumerates Barty's virtues:

He was in reality the simplest, the most affectionate, and most good-natured of men, the very soul of honor, the best of husbands and fathers and friends, the most fascinating companion that ever lived, and one who kept to the last the freshness and joyous spirits of a schoolboy and the heart of a child; one who never said or did an unkind thing; probably never even thought one. Generous and open-handed to a fault, slow to condemn, quick to forgive, and gifted with a power of immediately inspiring affection and keeping it forever after, such as I have never known in any one else, he grew to be (for all his quick-tempered impulsiveness) one of the gentlest and meekest and most humble-minded of men! (1-2)

Throughout the novel as well Maurice breathlessly proclaims his hero's deeds and thoughts to be the greatest he has ever encountered. The fact that this hero-worship comes from one who is wise in the ways of the world, a successful businessman and member of Parliament, reinforces the fantasy that even those who are interested in money and politics will pay homage to the handsome, athletic dreamer.

Barty Josselin is clearly a version of what Du Maurier himself desired to be. He is a fantasy figure so perfect that when we get a rare glimpse of him in the midst of despair—as when he is planning suicide because he thinks he will lose the sight in both eyes—we are shocked at his behavior. In fact, it takes the sudden intervention of Martia to put this near-perfect hero back on the pathway to success and glory. By grafting realistic autobiographical details onto this larger-than-life hero, Du Maurier creates an unsettling effect. The modern reader, conditioned by works such as Edwin Arlington Robinson's "Richard Cory," expects Bob Maurice's idol, like the secretly despondent Cory, to harbor a private grief or flaw that will eventually do him in. But, alas, Martia hides the cyanide pills and Barty goes on to win even more laurels than he has already gathered. He has only this one physical defect—blindness in one eye—but his character is never tarnished. One might even understand his suicidal thoughts in light of that suddenly acquired defect. If his body, like his beautiful character, cannot be whole, then it must be destroyed as an imperfect work of art. Du Maurier's compulsive idealism and romanticism, his hatred of the ugly and the misshappen, are vividly present in the characters of both Barty and Maurice. The former embodies the ideals of physical and spiritual beauty and the latter worships their embodiment.

The major theme of *The Martian* is the quest for aesthetic perfection. It is not a theme that most modern readers find congenial, and this is perhaps one reason why it is ranked the lowest of Du Maurier's three novels by the few critics who even choose to mention it.[10] Still, it is a theme that runs through Du Maurier's own life and helps to account for why he spent so much time in writing and rewriting *The Martian* and for why he considered it his best work. The story of his life, from his parents' instilling in him a love of beautiful music, people, and society, to his drawings in *Punch* of the elegant upper classes, with their tall handsome men and women, consisted of a search for beauty, for a worldly aesthetic that would give his life shape and meaning. He saw the world as comprised of the ugly and the beautiful and tolerated very few shades of gray between that black and white image. Du Maurier's conservatism, furthermore, fostered a hatred of change. In his mind beauty was equated with permanence and change was the worm that threatened to destroy it.

In his novels the beautiful can be found in Passy, in the persons of Madame Seraskier, and the duchess of Towers, in the character and transformed voice of Trilby, in the features of Leah and Marty, and in the whole being of Barty Josselin. Ugliness, on the other hand, is much less in evidence in his fiction but notable examples can be seen in Pentonville, in the features and morals of Colonel Ibbetson and Svengali, and, to some extent, in Bob Maurice, a Philistine with a crooked nose and other physical defects that Du Maurier will not allow the reader to forget. His novels can also be seen as contrasting permanence with change. In *Peter Ibbetson* Passy becomes the symbol of timeless beauty that is preserved through the art of dreaming true. In actuality, of course, the small village is horribly changed over the years. In *Trilby* the main characters are gradually brought to grief as they move away from the joyful and innocent days at the atelier. And in *The Martian* the most traumatic change that nearly wrecks the beautiful Barty Josselin is the loss of his sight in one eye. Like his hero, Du Maurier suffered the identical loss, but unlike Barty who transcends his disability, Du Maurier was forced to abandon his career as a serious painter and turned to illustration.

What makes this last novel different from the first two is that the theme of the search for the beautiful has been raised to a much higher pitch. One is accustomed to heroes like Oedipus, Macbeth, or Clym Yeobright in the *The Return of the Native*, who, for all their greatness, must struggle against their human frailty. Barty Josselin does not have much to battle against except his one physical defect. He is more of a symbol of aesthetic excellence than a literary character. He is Du Maurier's beautiful man who is never reduced to the level of common humanity. He moves through the novel growing toward a perfection that he finally achieves in death when he is reunited with the spirit of Martia. A closer look at Du Maurier's beautiful man and the theme of aesthetic perfection may shed some light on the author's idiosyncratic view of the world.

Du Maurier's beautiful man is a curious amalgam of machismo— found in the rugged characters of Robert Louis Stevenson, William Henley, and Rudyard Kipling—and of aesthetic sensibility as represented in the conclusion of Walter Pater's *The Renaissance*. Barty Josselin's life may be seen as a dramatic response to this passage from Pater:

A counted number of pulses only is given to us of a variegated, dramatic life. How may we see in them all that is to be seen in them by the finest senses? How shall we pass most swiftly from point to point, and be present always at the focus where the greatest number of vital forces unite in their purest energy?[11]

Like Peter Ibbetson, Barty inherits the sensibilities of two nationalities and two classes. Although he is a bastard, his parents were said to be "the handsomest couple in Paris." His mother was the daughter of "poor fisher folk" but they were "physically splendid people." Later she was carefully educated in music and passed onto her son both her physical beauty and musical talent. Barty's father, being a lord, instilled in him a refined sensibility and good taste. Barty is said to possess an angelic beauty, to be almost too handsome for a man. From youth he exhibited numerous talents—he could draw, sing French and English songs, play various musical instruments, see the satellites of Jupiter with his naked eye, hear a watch tick in the next room, and locate the north when blindfolded. He admired great physical strength and was himself an accomplished boxer, swimmer, and gymnast. Throughout his youth he was never ill a day nor did he ever experience an ache or a pain.

One observation about his physical prowess subtly anticipates his relationship with Martia and a higher race of being. Maurice says that Barty was "all but amphibious, and reminded me of the seal at the *Jardin des Plantes*." He seemed to spend all afternoon under water, "coming up to breathe now and then at unexpected moments, with a stone in his mouth that he had picked up from the slimy bottom ten or twelve feet below—or a weed—or a dead mussel" (48). It will be recalled that later in the novel Martia explains that man in Mars is amphibious and "seems to be something between our seal and our sea-lion," and that he feeds exclusively "on edible moss and roots and submarine seaweed" (366). Not only does the young Barty resemble a Martian, anticipating the evolution of his species, but the fact that his mother came from a people that worked the sea for their living suggests another kinship with the underwater Martians. He spends his vacation among whalers and fishermen, and Maurice reports that "he was always fond of that class; possibly also some vague atavistic sympathy for the toilers of the sea lay dormant in his blood like an inherited memory" (104).

Barty is totally attuned to the flow of life around him and is such a physical creature that he is compared to a squirrel, a collie pup, and a kitten, "with an immense appetite for food and fun and frolic." His knowledge of the world grows during his years as a Grenadier Guard and he develops an artist's sense of physical beauty that tolerates no imperfecton. He tells Maurice, "You've got a kink in your nose, Bob—if it weren't for that you'd be a deuced good-looking fellow—like me; but you ain't" (133). He goes on to note that the "kink" in his birth is "as big a killjoy as I know," since it keeps him from becoming the Marquis of Whitby. Physical beauty and social class become blended in his mind. He can admire the beauty in people of the lower class but oddly enough they turn out to look like Du Maurier's aristocrats: tall, statuesque, and refined thoroughbreds, one and all. Ugliness was, by and large, confined to the middle classes, a group of people Barty came to despise: "it was his theory

that all successful business people were pompous and purse-proud and
vulgar" (155). "The only men he couldn't stand," we are told, were
"the Philistines and the prigs—or both combined" (394). In Du
Maurier's novels and drawings the ugly character of this class is
reflected in its distorted features. Bob Maurice, who proclaims himself a Philistine, acknowledges his imperfection: "I'm no Adonis
myself. I've got a long upper lip and an Irish kink in my nose" (375).

It is Barty's philosophy that only the beautiful and gifted people
should propagate their kind. These people are to be found among the
Bohemians, the barbarians, and the proletariat. Du Maurier is bor-
rowing Matthew Arnold's classification of society, the Barbarians
(aristocrats), Philistines (middle class), and Populace (lower class),
but offers no program for educating or elevating the middle class.
Rather, Barty recommends the theory of selective breeding that
promises to weed out of future generations the vulgar, ugly, and
socially ambitious middle class. Bob Maurice, for example, accepts
Barty's theory and consequently is proud of his bachelorhood: "Any-
how, I have known my place. I have not perpetuated that kink, and
with it, possibly, the base and cowardly instincts of which it was
meant to be the outward and visible sign" (376).

Barty Josselin would have the world become brave, new, and
beautiful through a process of selective breeding. Du Maurier may
have acquired this idea from Sir Francis Galton, a pioneer in the study
of heredity, whose best-known book, *Inquiries into Human Faculty*,
was published in 1883. The equation of social class with good looks
was also common at this time, as witnessed in Du Maurier's own
visual stereotypes. Bob Maurice proclaims Barty's triumphal eugenics: "And to whom but Barty Josselin do we owe it that our race is on
an average already from four to six inches taller than it was thirty years
ago, men and women alike; that strength and beauty are rapidly
becoming the rule among us, and weakness and ugliness the exception?" Du Maurier here combines the ideals of Pater and Stevenson,
but goes well beyond them in advocating through eugenics a way to
maintain and intensify the hard gemlike flame of beauty and strength
through the centuries. "Who in these days," Maurice goes on,
"would dare to enter the holy state of wedlock unless they were
pronounced physically, morally, and mentally fit—to procreate their

kind—not only by their own conscience, but by the common consent of all who know them?" (375).

Within the character of Barty Josselin, then, Du Maurier has posited all the traits he himself desired, and some of which he possessed, that he would like to see develop and expand in subsequent generations. He is physically strong, tall, handsome, a major author, a fine artist and musician, a loving father and husband, a good friend; he combines the best features of the English and the French, the upper and lower classes—in short, he is the beautiful man upon whom a goddesslike creature descends to insure that, like a new Adam, he multiplies his kind and becomes the archetype for a world that is deliberate, beautiful, and a permanent work of art. Barty "has restored that absolute conviction of an indestructible germ of Immortality within us, born of remembrance made perfect and complete after dissolution. . . . Whatever the future may be, the past will be ours forever" (374).

Transcending the Senses

Behind the characterization of Barty Josselin and the theme of aesthetic perfection is Du Maurier's very human and overpowering fear of blindness. The well-worn adage that beauty lies in the eye of the beholder takes on new meaning to a man who believes that he is going blind. The loss of sight to Du Maurier was not simply a physical imperfection—like the kink in Bob Maurice's nose—but the annihilation of color, form, texture, proportion—all the qualities that he celebrates in his novels, drawings, and painting. It is no surprise, then, to find Barty Josselin begin in earnest to develop and form his career and philosophy after he loses the sight in one eye. Up to that point he was indulging his senses and sensibilities in the flux of experiences he enjoyed in France, England, and Belgium. "Present always at the focus where the greatest number of vital forces unite in their purest energy," he was living according to the Cyrenaic code that made pleasure the chief goal of life. With the sudden darkness in one eye came a period of numbing stillness, then despair, then introspection, and finally a rebirth of vitality and a coherent design for the future. This is the same structure of many great works of the period, including *Sartor Resartus*, *In Memoriam*, and "The Palace of Art."

In the first part of the novel Barty is the epicurean enjoying fine food and music, painting, literature, beautiful women, witty conversation, sports, tobacco, and a variety of friendships. He "had innocently gloried all his life in the singular perfection of his five wits" (208). In Antwerp Barty becomes friends with a polyglot named Tescheles who comes from a famous musical family. Tescheles introduces him to the music of Chopin, Liszt, Wagner, and Schumann, "music that ravished his soul with a novel enchantment" (188). Like the Soul in "The Palace of Art," Barty has by this time indulged all his senses to the full. We are told that "he was happier than he had ever been in his life" (189). Such a personal hedonism, an aesthetic of the mutable senses, has in it the seed of its own destruction. Here is the turning point of the novel as Barty heads for a fall, one that educates him to see the need of a beauty that is permanent and that transcends the Cyrenaic philosophy of Pater.

Despite his happiness in Antwerp, Barty becomes plagued with a desire to regain a consciousness of the north. The absence of that sensation, especially at night, "would send a chill thrill of desolation through him like a wave; a wild panic, a quick agony, as though the true meaning of absolute loneliness were suddenly realized by a lightning flash of insight, and it were to last forever and forever" (189). Then, one morning when he was painting in a studio along with a dozen other students the horror befell him: "whatever he looked at with the left [eye] dwindled to a vanishing point and became invisible. No rubbing or bathing of his eye would alter the terrible fact, and he knew what great fear really means, for the first time" (189). The narrator concludes this chapter with an observation that underscores the psychological theme of rebirth: "And then he was nearing the end of the time when he was to remain as other mortals are. His new life was soon to open, the great change to which we owe the Barty Josselin who had changed the world for *us*!" (190).

Like Du Maurier himself, Barty goes through a series of misleading medical diagnoses of his condition that raise and then dash his hopes for continued vision. Soon a veil seemed to come over his good eye: "by daylight he could see through this veil, but every object he saw was discolored and distorted and deformed—it was worse than darkness itself" (208). The delicate shapes, colors, and proportions of the world that had delighted him for all these years now form a grotesque parody of remembered beauty and threaten to shut themselves forever behind the veil. His generous and affable spirit is reduced to one of jealousy and self-pity: "thus in the unutterable utterness of his dejection he would make himself such evil cheer that he sickened with envy at the mere sight of any living thing that could see out of two eyes—a homeless irresponsible dog, a hunchback beggar, a crippled organ-grinder and his monkey" (209).

As the months pass, however, Barty's condition leads to his acquiring a finer morality. Bob Maurice offers a number of moral reflections upon one's living under the shadow of the sword of Damocles: "It rids one of much superfluous self-complacency and puts a wholesome check on our keeping too good a conceit of ourselves; it prevents us from caring too meanly about mean things—too keenly about our own infinitesimal personalities: it makes us feel quick sympathy for those who live under a like condition" (209 – 10). Barty's aunt, Lady Caroline Grey, comes to live with him to nurse him back to physical and mental health. He acknowledges his transformation to her: "I am a very altered person, and a very unlucky one" (212). She succeeds in nourishing his fading appetite for life by reading him famous works of literature, inviting people like l'Abbé Lefebvre and Father Louis to discuss politics or play classical music for him. Despite the reinfusion of culture and lively people into his life, Barty remains like Browning's Saul, in the grip of an overpowering depression, and about whom David says, "he lets me praise life, / Gives assent, yet would die for his own part."[12] Barty "would half sincerely long for death, of which he yet had such a horror that he was often tempted to kill himself to get the bother of it well over at once." He was absolutely appalled at the prospect of "death in the dark" (234).

Barty's despair is intensified by his gruesome encounter with the priest oculist in Louvain. Patting a small Italian greyhound that "lay and shivered and whined in a little round cot by the fire," the oculist tells Barty, "I hope you will have more fortitude than another young patient of mine (also an artist) to whom I was obliged to make a similar communication. He blew out his brains on my door-step!" He convinces Barty that he will lose the vision in his good eye, fondles his little greyhound, takes Barty to the door, "most politely bowing with his black velvet skull-cap; and pocketed his full fee (ten francs) with his usual grace of careless indifference, and gently shut the door on him" (249).

The next step in Barty's development is the total denial of life. He cannot accept himself as an imperfect and impaired creature that will be closed forever from all of the beautiful forms that comprised his earlier sensual existence. There is no romanticizing blindness in an artist as there might be in an intellectual or literary giant like Homer, Milton, or Joyce. For Barty heaven is a visual arrangement of lovely forms and hell is its absence. So he steals some cyanide of potassium from a photographic studio and prepares to take his own life. The description that follows is so precise in its details that one suspects that Du Maurier himself might have given serious thought to a similar attempt:

The cyanide was slow in melting. He crushed it angrily with his pen-holder—and the scent of bitter-almonds filled the room. . . .

He lay staring at the tumbler, watching little bubbles, revelling in what remained of his exquisite faculty of minute sight—with a feeling of great peace; and thought prayerfully; lost himself in a kind of formless prayer without words—lost himself completely. It was as if the wished-for dissolution were coming of its own accord; Nirvana—an ecstasy of conscious annihilation—the blessed end, the end of all! (254).

It is at this point that Martia intervenes to save his life. A knock comes to the door but no one is there, and when he returns to his bed he discovers the cyanide gone and a letter in Blaze from Martia.

Like the persona of *In Memoriam*, Barty's soul continues to grow, having come through the denial of life itself toward the final conquest of doubt and despair. By painful stages, he learns to transcend an isolating self-consciousness to become a vital link in a greater race of people. Through Martia, whether a fiction of his brain or an actual creature, he can rise above the paralysis of private grief, a state of numbing inactivity that is comparable to death, to reach a spiritual and aesthetic communion with both the beautiful undersea people that were his ancestors and the super race that he and Leah will produce who will perfect his seed "forever and ever beyond the stars" (406). "Once more," the reader is told, "life was full of hopes and possibilities" (259). Barty goes on to share his hopes with countless people through his inspired philosophy that argues for the perfection of mankind and the immortality of the soul.

The only peculiarity of Barty's teaching is his attitude toward suicide. The narrator observes that "through him suicide has become the normal way out of our troubles when these are beyond remedy." Apparently Bob Maurice is distressed at this particular influence of Barty's philosophy, for he says "I will not express my opinion as to the ethical significance of this admitted result of his teaching, which many of us still find it so hard to reconcile with their conscience" (374). The implication of Barty's advocacy of suicide seems to be that severely troubled people do themselves and the race a favor by ending their lives. They can end their suffering, enjoy their immortality in a new form, and free the race of their imperfection all at once. Since Barty, like Du Maurier, is an agnostic who enjoys upsetting the complacency of doctrinaire Christians, his rather shocking attitude toward suicide is meant to make the reader weigh the morality of unrelieved suffering against that of self-murder. In terms of the structure of the novel and its theme this small paragraph is largely irrelevant. Still, it is characteristic of Du Maurier in all his novels to insert little barbs and thrusts at groups of people and institutions he does not admire.

The Dual Fantasy

If Barty Josselin is Du Maurier's beautiful man, the embodiment of his social and aesthetic ideals, a character who moves through the archetypal stages of death and rebirth, and grows from a self-centered epicurean to a prophet of universal perfection—then Bob Maurice is Du Maurier's good ordinary man, a constant foil to Barty's character. Maurice represents the solid middle class which Du Maurier disliked and sought to rise above by whatever means were open to him. At the outset of the novel Maurice says, "My life is so full of Barty Josselin that I can hardly be said to have ever had an existence apart from his;

and I can think of no easier or better way to tell Barty's history than just telling my own" (3). This is an interesting comment for it reveals the basic autobiographical duality of the entire novel. Du Maurier has divided his own personality, the reality and the dream, between his two main characters. Some of the specific parallels between his own life and those of Barty and Maurice have already been drawn. In terms of straightforward autobiographical detail, both characters incorporate Du Maurier's experiences, but there is a clear division between the beautiful man, already discussed, and the good ordinary man. A similar representation of what might have been and what was can be seen in the hero of Henry James's partly autobiographical short story, "The Jolly Corner," published in 1908.

Bob Maurice is a self-acknowledged Philistine, a member of the respectable middle class. He has an apologetic whimsicality about himself that adds to his believability and charm. He refers to himself as "a mere prosperous tradesman, and busy politician and man of the world" (2). One of his great joys is to recall the bright and happy school days he spent with Barty. Like Peter Ibbetson, his favorite sport is "the pursuit of childhood memories." His hero-worship of Barty combined with his own self-effacement leads him to wait until the near end of the novel to give a brief account of his own life. It is interesting to note that in the six pages given to Maurice's own story Du Maurier manages to present an affectionate, disarmingly honest, and very likeable character—even though he is a member of the very class that Barty and Du Maurier spurn. In the character of Bob Maurice, Du Maurier was able to create a man so comfortable at home in his station of life and so aware of his limitations that he stands apart from the petty bourgeois and becomes an admirable figure, a sort of model Ordinary Man. Du Maurier hated prigs, effeminate men, aesthetes, and the petty ambitions, vulgarity, and avarice of the Philistines. Bob Maurice holds a similar point of view. He delays the story of Barty at one point to declare his disgust with prigs, whom he sees as the true Philistines. Later he asserts that "like Barty, I am fond of men's society; but at least I like them to be unmistakably men of my own sex, manly men, and clean." He belittles a group of aesthetes that earlier had come to study under Barty the artist by referring to them as the little clique of "misshapen troglodytes with foul minds and perverted passions" (327).

Maurice's attitude toward himself and his achievements reveals a bold, honest, and sometimes ironic mind: "The Right Honorable Sir Robert Maurice, Bart., M.P., etc., etc., etc. That's me. I take up a whole line of manuscript. I might be a noble lord if I chose, and take up two!" (412). The deadly seriousness with which a person of that class and prominence would typically take himself is here neatly undercut. Maurice is proud of his title but not ridiculously so. He has, mirabile dictu, a sense of humor, and that goes a long way in redeeming him in both the reader's and Du Maurier's eyes. Lacking a foolish sense of self-importance, Maurice reveals through his sense of humor a respect for the hierarchy of human values. He defines himself according to conventional and unconventional categories: "I am a liberal conservative, an opportunist, a pessi-optimist, an in-medio-tutissimist, and attend divine service at the Temple Church." He then proceeds to break through the prejudicial term "Philistine" to illustrate its inadequacy for filing human beings: "I'm a Philistine, and not ashamed; so was Molière—so was Cervantes. So, if you like, was the late Martin Farquhar Tupper—and those who read him; we're of all sorts in Philistia, the great and the small, the good and the bad" (412).

He knows his human limitations but enjoys life as fully as he can. He gracefully accepts the strength and good looks that remain in his aging body: "I'm in the sixties—sound of wind and limb—only two false teeth—one at each side, bicuspids, merely for show. I'm rather bald, but it suits my style; a little fat, perhaps—a pound and a half over sixteen stone! but I'm an inch and a half over six feet, and very big-boned" (412). As a prosperous wine merchant he is dedicated to the good life, one of pleasure in moderation. "What a prosperous and happy life mine has been," he exclaims. "Yes, I have warmed both hands at the fire of life, and even burnt my fingers now and then but not severely" (412). The loss of his parents and disappointment in love are among his few griefs in sixty years of hearty living.

Having established a credible, affable, and successful member of the middle class, Du Maurier proceeds to have Maurice defend the shopkeeping class and to point out the dangers inherent when human goals are exchanged for monetary ones: "To amass wealth is an engrossing pursuit—and now that I have amassed a good deal more than I quite know what to do with, it seems to me a very ignoble one. It chokes up everything that makes life worth living" (415). Still, despite his fortune, Maurice knows that he has done better things and that money was the source of his higher accomplishments: "I have helped to govern my country and make its laws; but it all came out of wine to begin with—all from learning how to buy and sell" (413).

Maurice is very self-conscious about his wealth and position in society. He is aware, for example, that "if I had been a failure Barty would have stuck to me like a brick, I feel sure, instead of my sticking to him like a leech!" (413). His lifelong cultivation of Barty's circle and that of his artistic friends, however, has also unfitted him for the society of his fellow wine merchants, not to mention the "leaders of intellectual modern thought," a group that is both depressed by and disgusted at Maurice's wealth. Because he is aware of the shortcomings of his class and maintains a proper humility and detachment, Maurice proves to be the good ordinary man. He admits toward the end of his brief account of his life that he would not choose to live his years over again. Still, he remains wonderfully human in his inconsistency when he asserts his desire to live twenty more years "if only to take Leah's unborn great-grandchildren to the dentist's and tip them at school, and treat them to the pantomime and Madame Tussaud's, as I did their mothers and grandmothers before them" (416).

Between Barty Josselin and Bob Maurice Du Maurier could share the best of two worlds. Like his hero, Du Maurier was a successful and sought after novelist, but unlike him, he was never able to cope with his sudden wealth and popularity. The practical world of lectures, fan mail, and the recurrent echoes of the *Trilby* boom overwhelmed and oppressed him. He was possessed by the past, and, now that he was living in Oxford Square, he revisited his old home in Hampstead, a calm haven that held pleasant memories of family gatherings. He lived close to London and to the public's constant demand for his attention, but in fact, he was a resident of a distant world—Passy, by way of Hampstead—a world, for all practical purposes, as remote as Mars but as intimate as a dream or a remembrance. Bob Maurice, on the other hand, is a man who copes exceedingly well with the practical world of business and who possesses a commonsense philosophy about middle-class values. To this extent he is as much of a fantasy of the aging, withdrawn Du Maurier as is Barty Josselin.

Du Maurier never really resolved the three major conflicts of his own life: his middle-class origins versus his aristocratic and bohemian longings; the world of practical affairs versus that of beautiful dreams; and the oppression of the present versus the freedom of the past. It is precisely these conflicts, however, that account for the duality in all of Du Maurier's novels. But here in *The Martian*, and for the first time, he draws a strong, admirable character of the middle class who can boast "I'm a Philistine, and am not ashamed" and still devote his life to his dreaming hero: "My life is so full of Barty Josselin that I can hardly be said to have ever had an existence apart from his." They never become one, however, despite all the protestations to that effect, but we see Du Maurier at the end of his career still trying to fuse together the two disparate worlds that comprised both his heritage and his legacy.

Chapter Six
Conclusion

In *The Art of England* (1887) John Ruskin, the most respected art critic of his day, offered this remarkable praise of Du Maurier's artistic talent:

the acute, highly trained, and accurately physiologic observation of Du Maurier traced for us, to its true origin in vice or virtue, every order of expression in the mixed circle of metropolitan rank and wealth: and has done so with a closeness of delineation the like of which has not been seen since Holbein, and deserving the most respectful praise in that, whatever power of satire it may reach by the selection and assemblage of telling points of character, it never degenerates into caricature.[1]

Like Henry James, who noted that Du Maurier's work in *Punch* constitutes "a complete comedy of manners,"[2] Ruskin discusses Du Maurier's achievements more in terms of literature than art. These two critics were concerned with the social meanings implicit in his drawings and with the personalities of the characters he depicted. Their focus seems to be a sound one, because Du Maurier, as was noted earlier, encroached upon the function of the novelist by using several fictitious characters repeatedly in his pictures, so that not only their appearance but their manners and their opinions and their homes and families became familiar to loyal readers of *Punch*: Mrs. Ponsonby de Tompkyns, Sir Gorgius Midas, Mrs. Cimabue Brown, Maudle, and Jellaby Postlethwaite—these and others became as well known in the 1880s as their stage equivalents at the Savoy—Major-General Stanley, Sir Joseph Porter, and Reginald Bunthorne. *Punch* was filled with clever and superbly drawn cartoons, but Du Maurier's especial achievement in the magazine was his creation of memorable satiric characters.

Du Maurier moved beyond the limits of the single sketch not only by his use of recurring characters but by his grouping of drawings in series with stated themes, such as "Things one would rather have left unsaid," "Things one would rather have expressed differently," "Social agonies," and "Feline amenities." His thirty years of work in *Punch* show him to be approaching the borderline that divides drawings with a verbal caption from a written text with illustrations. It is in light of that strong literary quality of Du Maurier's drawings that admirers of his work like James and Ruskin acknowledge his achievements as an artist.

Besides having "reproduced every possible situation that is likely to be encountered in the English novel of manners,"[3] as James observed, Du Maurier's drawings also extended the art of the grotesque. Although working within the nineteenth-century visual tradition epitomized in the drawings of Cruikshank, Du Maurier also reflects the influence of Hieronymus Bosch in his nightmare cartoons depicting a two-headed monster, men smoking out of their own brain pans, and a black spider with a human head. These works, along with his idyllic, dreamlike scenes in Hampstead, show Du Maurier's experimental interest in the world of dreams and the psychology of the unconscious, subjects he was to explore further in his novels.

Simply in terms of the visual impact of his drawings, Du Maurier's precise lines, and especially his careful grouping of figures, influenced the work of other illustrators and artists. Even the famous John Millais acknowledged his debt to Du Maurier's illustrations in helping to place his own figures in a painting.[4] It is Du Maurier's tall, stately woman, however, that had the greatest influence upon other artists and, perhaps, even upon fashions. Her creator unashamedly announces that

She is my pièce de résistance, and I have often heard her commended, and the praise of her has sounded sweet in mine ears, and gone straight to my heart, for she has become to me as a daughter. She is rather tall, I admit, and a trifle stiff; but Englishwomen *are* tall and stiff just now, and she is rather too serious. . . . And as for the height, I have often begun by drawing the dear creature *little*, and found that by one sweep of the pen (adding a few inches to the bottom of her skirt) I have improved her so much that it has been impossible to resist the temptation.[5]

Du Maurier's drawings may well have been instrumental in bringing the tall woman into fashion toward the end and turn of the century. It has been jokingly asserted that he permanently raised the height of the typical English girl by several inches. In America, the popular illustrator Charles Dana Gibson created the famous "Gibson Girl" of the 1890s, an idealized figure typically dressed in a tailored shirtwaist with leg-of-mutton sleeves, and a long skirt. A bit more perky than Du Maurier's serious woman, she nevertheless bears her unmistakable imprint. Later in the period, *Punch* artist Bernard Partridge continued to supply drawings in the Du Maurier style but his work was not as good as Du Maurier's. Still, he kept the tall, beautiful Victorian woman alive well into the twentieth century.

Given the literary quality of his cartoons and his close association with novelists as their illustrator, one may view Du Maurier's own novels as an extension and analysis of his artistic vision. His accomplishments as a novelist are many. Despite the fact that he wrote only three novels, lacking the variety of Dickens and the polish of James, his contribution to the art of the novel has been largely ignored. Du Maurier's novels defied the conventional prudery of the times by exhibiting a new candor in accord with the fiction of George Moore and the translations of Zola. His works contain many unconventional details that shocked his Victorian readers: Trilby's posing in the nude and being the mistress of several men before offering herself to Little Billee; Little Billee's outspoken agnosticism that caused an angry quarrel with a clergyman; and Barty Josselin's illegitimate birth and promiscuous sex affairs as a young man.

Du Maurier also reshaped the traditional romantic novel. As Lionel Stevenson observed, "Du Maurier's novels unmistakably belong to the category of romantic fiction, but in a special way that distinguishes them from all the other books. . . . he adapted the attributes of the romantic tradition to suit the mood of a new epoch."[6] The most conspicuous element in his three books that was almost exclusively his own was his persistent probing of the unconscious mind. Memory, dreams, hypnotism, free association, and automatic writing are the five phenomena that constitute the range of psychological interest in the unconscious exhibited in the novels. Du Maurier does not seem to have been aware that in the very years he was writing, some of the most innovative philosophers and scientists were investigating the same mental phenomena that formed the heart of his novels. Sigmund Freud was experimenting with hypnotism in connection with his study of aphasia. Later he studied the process of free association, as revealed in dreams. Henri Bergson in 1895 published *Matière et mémoire*, in which he argues that memory provides the only true continuity to human existence. In that same year Gertrude Stein conducted experiments with automatic writing in the laboratory of William James.

Du Maurier possessed an uncanny sense of his times and explored the subject of the unconscious in terms of one major theme—the split personality. Peter Ibbetson, Trilby, and Barty Josselin each exhibits a fundamental duality in personality. Their minds move between dream and reality. Peter conducts his life for years on two different levels, that of dreams and that of everyday consciousness. Trilby develops a totally new personality under Svengali's hypnotic influence. And Barty Josselin has his normal faculties suspended during sleep and is possessed by a foreign intelligence that communicates through his automatic writing. The dominant theme of the double in the Victorian novel and poetry is here explored in detail. Robert Louis Stevenson, in *The Strange Case of Dr. Jekyll and Mr. Hyde* (1886), is one of the few authors who previously had treated the theme of the split personality in such dramatic detail.

Besides his modernity in probing of the unconscious mind and developing the theme of the double personality, Du Maurier also embodied in his novels the gospel of Walter Pater: "To burn always with this hard, gem-like flame, to maintain this ecstasy, is success in life."[7] All of Du Maurier's heroes and heroines, even his villains, for that matter, possess finely tuned sensibilities that lead them to ecstatic responses to beauty, whether found in poetry, painting, music, the human body, or even in smells and taste. All of his novels reveal the romantic quest after an ideal and ineffable beauty—and anticipate the theme of William Butler Yeats's "Sailing to Byzantium" and James Joyce's notion of an epiphany. The French critic, Maurice Lanoire, is correct in seeing as Du Maurier's leading motif, "the need to flee the reality in the dream as one approaches death."[8]

Lionel Stevenson is one of the few critics of our day who has recognized Du Maurier's role in the development of the novel. Calling his works "masterpieces of romantic fiction," Stevenson goes on to say that

The unprecedented popular appeal of Du Maurier's novels begins to be understandable when one realizes how many different strands of interest, both new and old, were woven into their apparently casual texture. Writing in the transitional decade of the nineties, he derived ingredients from the accumulated fiction of the whole nineteenth century, and instinctively combined them with current ideas that were to develop into the major innovations of the twentieth.[9]

Stevenson is exactly right in his assessment of Du Maurier's unique contribution to the history of the novel. To the old elements of romantic fiction—its nostalgia, heroics, love affairs, adventure, and melodrama—Du Maurier added new and contemporary ideas of the unconscious mind, the double personality, the ideals of aestheticism, and sexual fantasy.

But Du Maurier's legacy goes beyond the intrinsic literary value of the works themselves. As L. Edward Purcell has shown, the publication of *Trilby* was a key factor in the development of the best-seller system. With the cheap reprint houses disappearing after the passage of the new copyright law in 1891, a few large publishers, most of whom were located in New York, obtained control of a growing industry. *Trilby* was the first of a new breed of "sellers," as they were then called, that were at the heart of the new publishing system. Publishers now exercised complete control over their books and their profits ran higher than ever before and their popular authors were assured of considerable wealth. As Purcell states, "Du Maurier's book was not the cause of the new system, but *Trilby* was the first great example of how the machinery of promotion, distribution, secondary rights, and social hoopla would work."[10]

Even more important and enduring than his innovative themes and his impact on the best-seller system is Du Maurier's creation of Svengali. If he had done nothing else, he would deserve immortality for thinking up that brilliant demonic character. Trilby may have won the hearts of the Victorians but Svengali conjured up their deepest unconscious fears and desires. Here was a man whose strange powers gave him complete control over a beautiful woman. Frightening and evil, yes, but at the same time Svengali represented an exhilarating freedom from the conventional moral and social restraints of the Victorian age. Fascinating and repulsive, creative and destructive, Svengali survives in the popular imagination to this day. Like Sherlock Holmes and Dr. Jekyll and Mr. Hyde, he is known by millions of people who never read the pages that first gave him breath to speak. He has become one of the classic villains and thus joins the ranks of Iago, Claggart, and Dr. Moriarity. He shares with them a background shrouded in mystery and a terrifying power to manipulate the fates of those around him. Black magician, Wandering Jew, malignant Orpheus, devil-god, and spider-cat—Svengali's paradoxical character is a rich composite of archetypes that will continue to touch our deepest emotions.

Notes and References

Chapter One

1. Quoted in Leonée Ormond, *George Du Maurier* (Pittsburgh, 1969), p. 4.
2. Ibid., p. 7.
3. Ibid., p. 8.
4. *Peter Ibbetson* (New York, 1891), p. 18.
5. Daphne Du Maurier, *The Du Mauriers* (London, 1937), p. 144.
6. Ibid., p. 160.
7. Ibid., p. 194.
8. Quoted in Du Maurier, *Du Mauriers*, p. 200.
9. *Peter Ibbetson*, p. 134.
10. Ibid., p. 161.
11. Robert H. Sherard, "The Author of *Trilby*," *McClure's Magazine* 4 (October, 1895):396.
12. *Peter Ibbetson*, p. 184.
13. *Trilby* (New York, 1894), p. 2.
14. Ibid., p. 3.
15. Ibid., p. 78.
16. Ormond, p. 44.
17. *The Young George Du Maurier*, ed. Daphne Du Maurier (London, 1951), following p. 176.
18. Quoted in Sherard, pp. 397−98.
19. Felix Moscheles, *In Bohemia with Du Maurier* (London, 1896), p. 47.
20. Unlike Ormond, Daphne Du Maurier in *The Du Mauriers* sees the relationship to be one of simple infatuation: "Kicky's sketchbooks were full of Carry at this time, and he wrote scraps of verses, too—*complete nonsense* —about himself and Moscheles fighting for her favours, and how she would marry one of them and love the other" (p. 273; italics mine).
21. From an account Du Maurier gave in *The George Eliot Letters*, ed. Gordon Haight (New Haven: Yale University Press, 1956), 7:60−61.
22. Du Maurier, *Young George Du Maurier*, p. 29.
23. Ibid., p. 112.
24. Ibid., pp. 44−45.
25. Ibid., p. 163.
26. Ibid., pp. 251−52.

27. Ormond, p. 184.

28. Quoted in ibid., p. 228.

29. Ibid., p. 248.

30. Henry James, "George Du Maurier," *Harper's New Monthly Magazine* 95 (September, 1897):594.

31. Ormond, p. 394.

32. Quoted in J. B. and J. L. Gilder, *Trilbyana* (New York, 1895), p. 12.

33. Quoted in Ormond, p. 466.

34. Quoted in ibid., p. 467.

35. Quoted in ibid., p. 471.

36. James, "George Du Maurier," *Harper's New Monthly Magazine*, pp. 608—9.

37. Ormond, p. 494.

Chapter Two

1. "The Illustration of Books from the Serious Artist's Point of View.—II," *Magazine of Art*, September, 1890, p. 374.

2. Ibid., p. 371.

3. Quoted in Sir Henry Lucy, *Sixty Years in the Wilderness* (New York, 1909), p. 391.

4. Henry James, "George Du Maurier," in *Partial Portraits* (London, 1899), p. 344.

5. Ibid., pp. 344—45.

6. Ibid., p. 357.

7. George Meredith, *The Egoist* (Boston: Houghton Mifflin, 1958), p. 11.

8. "A Legend of Camelot," pt. 2, 50 (March 10, 1866):97.

9. Walter Pater, *The Renaissance* (London: Macmillan, 1910), p. 236.

10. For a fuller treatment of this subject, see Roy McMullen, *Victorian Outsider: A Biography of J. A. M. Whistler* (New York, 1973), pp. 113—29.

11. *Punch* 66 (May 2, 1874):189.

12. *Punch* 79 (October 30, 1880):194.

13. *Punch* 78 (February 14, 1880):66.

14. *Punch* 79 (July 17, 1880):23.

15. *Punch* 79 (December 25, 1880):294.

16. *Punch* 80 (February 12, 1881):62.

17. J. A. M. Whistler, *The Gentle Art of Making Enemies*, ed. Sheridan Ford (New York, 1890), p. 241.

18. Oscar Wilde, "The Decay of Lying," in *Intentions* (London: Methuen, 1899), p. 6.

19. *Punch* 79 (October 9, 1880):167.

20. *Punch* 80 (May 21, 1881):229.

21. "Ponsonby de Tompkyns Begins to Assert Himself," *Punch* 81 (July 23, 1881):30.

22. James, *Partial Portraits*, p. 366.

23. M. H. Spielmann and L. S. Layard, *Kate Greenaway* (New York, 1968), p. 205.

24. *Punch* 74 (February 9, 1878):58.

25. *Punch*, "Almanack," 87 (December 9, 1884).

26. *Punch* 78 (May 15, 1880):222.

27. "Music at Home—With A Vengeance," *Punch* 83 (July 8, 1882):6.

28. Ormond, p. 338.

29. James, *Partial Portraits*, p. 350.

30. *Punch* 76 (February 15, 1879):66.

31. *Punch* 79 (October 23, 1880):186.

32. *Punch* 87 (August 23, 1884):86.

33. James, *Partial Portraits*, p. 361.

34. *Punch* 73 (August 11, 1877):54.

35. *Punch* 63 (August 3, 1872):48.

36. *Trilby* (New York, 1894), p. 259.

37. "Things One Would Rather Have Left Unsaid," *Punch* 95 (December 8, 1888):267.

38. "True Humility," *Punch* 109 (November 9, 1885):222.

39. "A Home Thrust," *Punch* 66 (June 13, 1874):248.

40. *Punch* 81 (December 10, 1881):220.

41. *Punch*, "Almanack," 79 (December, 1880).

42. "Heard in Mid-Atlantic," *Punch* 84 (February 3, 1883):51.

43. *Punch* 97 (August 31, 1889):97.

44. *Punch* 79 (December 11, 1880):270.

45. "Men Were Deceivers Ever," *Punch* 89 (November 21, 1885):246.

46. *Punch* 63 (September 14, 1872):113.

47. *Punch* 73 (December 22, 1877):279.

48. *Punch* 66 (January 24, 1874):38.

49. "Extremes that Meet," *Punch* 66 (March 14, 1874):110.

50. *Punch* 68 (April 3, 1875):150.

51. "Female Clubs vs. Matrimony," *Punch*, "Almanack," 74 (December, 1880).

52. "The Height of Magnificence," *Punch* 78 (February 7, 1880):59.

53. "All in the Day's Work," *Punch* 72 (June 30, 1877):294.

54. *Punch* 96 (May 4, 1889): 210.

55. *Punch* 79 (January 1, 1881): 306.

56. *Punch* 66 (June 20, 1874):263.

57. *Trilby*, p. 142.

58. *The Martian* (New York, 1897), p. 412.

59. *Trilby*, p. 286.

60. *Peter Ibbetson* (New York, 1891), p. 117.

61. *Punch* 82 (May 20, 1882):238.

62. *Punch* 68 (March 6, 1875):99.

63. *Punch* 64 (June 14, 1873):244.

64. "Hasty Generalization," *Punch* 75 (September 7, 1878):107.

65. *Punch* 64 (May 3, 1873):182.

66. *Punch* 55 (December 26, 1868):272.

67. The Jenkins cartoons appeared untitled in *Punch* 54 (February 1, 15, 22, 29, 1868):50, 70, 87, 89, respectively.

68. *Punch* 56 (January 16, 1869):21.

69. "Social Pictorial Satire. Part II," *Harper's New Monthly Magazine* 96 (March, 1898):516.

70. Ibid.

71. Ibid.

72. James, *Partial Portraits*, p. 356.

Chapter Three

1. Spielmann and Layard, p. 205.

2. Henry James, "George Du Maurier," *Harper's Weekly Magazine* 38 (April, 1894):341.

3. *Peter Ibbetson* (New York, 1891), p. 12; hereafter cited in the text.

4. Gilder, *Trilbyana*, pp. 12−13.

5. Lionel Stevenson, "George Du Maurier and the Romantic Novel," in *Essays by Divers Hands*, ed. N. Hardy Wallis (London, 1960), p. 42.

6. William Gaunt, *The Pre-Raphaelite Dream* (New York, 1966), pp. 40−41.

7. Lionel Stevenson, p. 43.

8. Pater, p. 236.

9. Sherard, pp. 393−94.

10. James, "George Du Maurier," *Harper's Weekly Magazine*, p. 342.

11. Ibid.

12. Ibid.

13. Ormond, p. 419.

14. Gilder, *Trilbyana*, p. 12.

15. Ormond, p. 425.

16. Edmund Wilson, "The Jews," in *A Piece of My Mind: Recollections at Sixty* (London, 1957), p. 80.

17. James, "George Du Maurier," *Harper's New Monthly Magazine*, p. 606.

18. Lionel Stevenson, p. 48.

19. James, "The Art of Fiction," in *Partial Portraits* pp. 384, 390.

20. Robert Louis Stevenson, "A Humble Remonstrance," *The Works of Robert Louis Stevenson* (New York, 1922), 12:211, 213.

21. Wilde, "The Decay of Lying," in *Intentions*, pp. 6, 8.

22. Lionel Stevenson, p. 51.

23. Ibid., p. 54.

24. Deems Taylor, introduction to *Peter Ibbetson* (New York, 1932), p. xiv.

Chapter Four

1. George Bernard Shaw, "Trilby and 'L' Ami des Femmes,'" in *Dramatic Opinions and Essays with an Apology by Bernard Shaw* (New York, 1922), 1:228.

2. James, "George Du Maurier," *Harper's New Monthly Magazine*, p. 603.

3. Luke Ionides, *Memoirs* (Paris, 1925), p. 63.

4. For a thorough and interesting account of the development of mesmerism, see Fred Kaplan's *Dickens and Mesmerism* (Princeton, 1975).

5. Ibid., p. 190.

6. Charles Dickens, *The Mystery of Edwin Drood*, (Oxford: Clarendon Press, 1972), pp. 53–54.

7. *Trilby* (New York, 1894), p. 60; hereafter cited in the text.

8. *Groves Dictionary of Music* (New York: St. Martin's Press, 1960), 6: 492. Permission to inter Paganini's body in consecrated ground was withheld until five years after his death because superstitious rumors claimed that he was in league with the devil.

9. James, "George Du Maurier," *Harper's New Monthly Magazine*, p. 605.

10. Ibid.

11. Edmund Wilson, "The Jews," in *A Piece of My Mind: Recollections at Sixty* (London, 1957), pp. 79–80.

12. Edgar Rosenberg, *From Shylock to Svengali* (Stanford, 1960), pp. 245–46.

13. Quoted in A. Bright, "Mr. Du Maurier at Home," *Idler* 8 (December 1895):421.

14. C. C. Hoyar Millar, *George Du Maurier and Others* (London, 1937), p. 154.

15. Shaw, p. 231.

16. Ibid.

17. Ibid., p. 232.

18. Ibid.

19. Ibid., p. 230.

20. Many of the details of Trilby-mania outlined here are derived from L. Edward Purcell's "Trilby and Trilby-Mania, The Beginning of the Bestseller System," *Journal of Popular Culture* 11 (Summer 1977):62− 76.

21. Isaac Hull Platt, *The Ethics of Trilby* (Philadelphia, 1895), pp. 4, 5, 10.

Chapter Five

1. Quoted in Ormond, p. 483.

2. Sherard, p. 400.

3. Ibid., p. 394.

4. *The Martian* (New York, 1897), p. 255; hereafter cited in the text.

5. Quoted in Lionel Stevenson, pp. 45−46.

6. Charles Darwin, *On the Origin of Species* (Cambridge: Harvard University Press, 1964), p. 490.

7. Alfred Lord Tennyson, "Epilogue" of *In Memoriam*, ed. Robert H. Ross (New York: W. W. Norton, 1973), ll. 124−130.

8. Rosenberg, pp. 234−61.

9. Ibid., p. 261.

10. Lionel Stevenson, Leonée Ormond, and Edgar Rosenberg all judge *The Martian* to be Du Maurier's least successful novel. In Stevenson's words, Du Maurier's "wish-fulfillments went too far" in his last novel (p. 53).

11. Pater, p. 236.

12. *The Complete Poetical Works of Browning*, ed. Horace E. Scudder (Cambridge: Houghton Mifflin, 1895), ll. 34−35.

Chapter Six

1. *The Art of England* in *The Works of John Ruskin*, eds. E. T. Cook and Alexander Wedderburn (London, 1908), 33:359.

2. James, in *Partial Portraits*, p. 357.

3. Ibid., p. 344.

4. Ormond, p. 357.

5. "The Illustration of Books," p. 372.

6. Lionel Stevenson, p. 51.

7. Pater, p. 236.

8. Maurice Lanoire, "Un Anglo-Français, Georges Du Maurier," *Revue de Paris* 47 (1940):278.

9. Lionel Stevenson, p. 48.

10. Purcell, p. 75.

Selected Bibliography

PRIMARY SOURCES

"The Illustration of Books from the Serious Artist's Point of View."
Magazine of Art, August, September, 1890, pp. 349–53, 371–75.
The Martian. New York: Harper and Brothers, 1897. Illustrated by the author.
Peter Ibbetson. New York: Harper and Brothers, 1891. Illustrated by the author.
"Recollections of an English Goldmine." *Once a Week* 5 (September 21, 1861): 356–64.
Society Pictures. 2 vols. London: Bradbury, Agnew, and Co., 1891.
Trilby. New York: Harper and Brothers, 1894. Illustrated by the author.
The Young George Du Maurier: A Selection of his Letters, 1860–67. Edited by Daphne Du Maurier. London: Peter Davies, 1951.

SECONDARY SOURCES

Brewster, Sir David. *More Worlds Than One*. New York: G. P. Putnam's Sons, n.d. A speculative account of intelligent life on other planets which may have influenced Du Maurier in writing *The Martian*.
Bright, Addison. "Mr. Du Maurier at Home." *Idler* 8 (December, 1895): 415–22. An interview with Du Maurier containing some lively observations and anecdotes.
Du Maurier, Daphne. *The Du Mauriers*. London: Victor Gollancz, 1937. An account of the Du Maurier family from 1810 to 1863, the date of George's marriage to Emma. Provides valuable insights into George's life but the fictionalized form of the book, with its imagined dialogue, weakens its reliability as factual biography.
Eliot, George. *The George Eliot Letters*. Edited by Gordon Haight. Vol. 7. New Haven: Yale University Press, 1956. Chronicles a few details of Eliot's and Lewes's friendship with Du Maurier.
Gaunt, William. *The Pre-Raphaelite Dream*. New York: Schocken Books,

1966. Provides helpful background information for understanding Du Maurier's aesthetics and satires.

Gilder, J. B., and Gilder, J. L. *Trilbyana: The Rise and Progress of a Popular Novel*. New York: Critic Co., 1895. A potpourri of information, some of it unique, about *Trilby*. Contains the following sections: "Trilby: a Novel"; Mr. Du Maurier as a Draughtsman; "Trilby" on the Stage; Personalia; Mr. Du Maurier and Mr. Whistler; "Trilby" entertainments; Miscellanea (letters, anecdotes, and Trilby fads); Songs; A Search for Sources; Nodier's "Trilby," le Lutin d'Argail; and seven illustrations.

Ionides, Luke. *Memoirs*. Paris: Privately printed, 1925. Contains a brief account of the visits of Du Maurier and other notables to Tulse Hill.

James, Henry. "Du Maurier and London Society." *Century Magazine* 36 (May, 1883):48−65. Reprinted in *Partial Portraits* (London: Macmillan and Co., 1899). One of the first serious and detailed discussions of Du Maurier's pictorial satire of society in *Punch*.

―――. "George Du Maurier." *Harper's New Monthly Magazine* 95 (September, 1897):594−609. James's personal reminiscences marked by insightful comments on Du Maurier's three novels.

―――. "George Du Maurier." *Harper's Weekly Magazine* 38 (April 14, 1894):341−42. A short but perceptive commentary on *Peter Ibbetson* and *Trilby*.

Kaplan, Fred. *Dickens and Mesmerism*. Princeton: Princeton University Press, 1975. Well-researched and informative account of the development of mesmerism in the early nineteenth century and its impact upon the novels of Dickens.

Lanoire, Maurice. "Un Anglo-Français, Georges Du Maurier." *Revue de Paris* 47 (1940):263−81. Says the major theme of Du Maurier's novels is the necessity to escape reality (and mortality) by entering the world of dreams.

Lucy, Henry W. *Sixty Years in the Wilderness*. New York: E. P. Dutton and Co., 1909. Contains a number of personal reminiscences about Du Maurier.

McMullen, Roy. *Victorian Outsider: A Biography of J. A. M. Whistler*. New York: E. P. Dutton and Co., 1973. Recounts Du Maurier's early friendship and subsequent disenchantment with the American artist.

Millar, C. C. Hoyer. *George Du Maurier and Others*. London: Cassell and Co., 1937. An interesting portrait of Du Maurier by his son-in-law.

Moscheles, Felix. *In Bohemia with Du Maurier*. London: T. F. Unwin, 1896. One of the rare sources of information about Du Maurier's days in Belgium from 1897 to 1859.

Ormond, Leonée. *George Du Maurier*. Pittsburgh: University of Pittsburgh Press, 1969. The definitive biography, profusely illustrated.

Platt, Isaac Hull. *The Ethics of Trilby: with a Supplemental Note on Spiritual Affinity*. Philadelphia: Conservator, 1895. This pamphlet argues that Trilby is spiritually pure and that a moral condemnation of her reflects a sexist double standard.

Purcell, L. Edward. "Trilby and Trilby-Mania, The Beginning of the Bestseller System." *Journal of Popular Culture* 11 (Summer 1977): 62–76. Traces the origin of the bestseller system to *Trilby* and details the marketing of Trilby products.

Rosenberg, Edgar. *From Shylock to Svengali*. Stanford: Stanford University Press, 1960. Contains an informative chapter on Du Maurier's depiction of the Jew in his novels. Focuses upon the character of Svengali but marred by flippant treatment of the novels.

Ruskin, John. *The Works of John Ruskin*. Edited by E. T. Cook and Alexander Wedderburn. Vol. 33. *The Art of England*. London: George Allen, 1908. A series of lectures delivered at Oxford containing several laudatory comments on Du Maurier's artistic achievements.

Shaw, George Bernard. "Trilby and 'L'Ami des Femmes.'" In *Dramatic Opinions and Essays with an Apology by Bernard Shaw*. New York: Brentano's, 1922, 1:228–36. A review of Beerbohm Tree's production of Paul Potter's stage version of *Trilby* at the Haymarket Theatre, October 30, 1895.

Sherard, Robert H. "The Author of Trilby." *McClure's Magazine* 4 (October, 1895):391–400. An interview with Du Maurier that is a valuable source of information about aspects of his life, writing, and drawings not revealed elsewhere.

Spielmann, M. H. *The History of Punch*. New York: Cassell Publishing Co., 1895. Definitive study of the first fifty-four years of the magazine.

———, and Layard, G. S. *Kate Greenaway*. New York: Benjamin Blom, 1968. Contains a brief account of her relationship with Du Maurier, her Hampstead neighbor.

Stevenson, Lionel. "George Du Maurier and the Romantic Novel." In *Essays by Divers Hands*, edited by N. Hardy Wallis. London: Oxford University Press, 1960. Argues persuasively that Du Maurier's novels are "masterpieces of romantic fiction."

Stevenson, Robert Louis. "A Humble Remonstrance." In *The Works of Robert Louis Stevenson*. Vol. 12. New York: Charles Scribner's Sons, 1922. An eloquent defense of romantic fiction, written in response to

James's "The Art of Fiction." Illuminates the critical milieu in which Du Maurier developed his own brand of romantic fiction.

Whistler, J. A. M. *The Gentle Art of Making Enemies*. Edited by Sheridan Ford. New York: F. Stokes and Bros., 1890. Recounts some of the artist's relationships with Du Maurier.

Whitely, **Derek Pepys**. *George Du Maurier*. London: Art and Technics, 1948. A brief account of Du Maurier's life and drawings. Contains a complete check list of books that he illustrated and several pencil studies nowhere else reproduced.

Wilson, **Edmund**. "The Jews." In *A Piece of My Mind: Recollections at Sixty*. London: W. H. Allen, 1957, pp. 64–103. Discusses the religious and literary character of the Jew in Du Maurier's novels.

Wood, **T. Martin**. *George Du Maurier—The Satirist of the Victorians: A Review of His Art and Personality*. London: Chatto and Windus, 1913. Especially valuable for its treatment of Du Maurier's art work before he joined *Punch* (illustrations of books and drawings for other periodicals).

BOOKS ILLUSTRATED BY DU MAURIER
(Place of publication for all is London)

The Book of Drawing-Room Plays, by Henry Dalton. Cassel, Petter, and Galpin, 1861. 4 illustrations.

Sylvia's Lovers, by Mrs. Gaskell. Smith, Elder, 1863. 5 illustrations including frontispiece and title page.

Cranford, by Mrs. Gaskell. Smith, Elder, 1864. 4 illustrations including title page.

Luke Ashleigh, by Alfred Elwes. Griffith and Farran, 1864. 6 illustrations.

English Sacred Poetry of the Olden Time. Religious Tract Society, 1864. 2 illustrations.

Lizzie Leigh, The Grey Woman, and Cousin Phillis, by Mrs. Gaskell. 1 vol. ed. Smith, Elder, 1865. 3 illustrations including title page.

Our Life Illustrated by Pen and Pencil. Religious Tract Society, 1865. 1 illustration.

Divine and Moral Songs, by Dr. Watts. Nisbet, 1865. 1 illustration.

Foxe's Book of Martyrs. Cassell, Petter, and Galpin, 1866. 1 illustration.

Lady Audley's Secret, by M. E. Braddon. Maxwell, 1866. 1 illustration used for jacket of "yellow back."

The Ingoldsby Legends, by R. H. Barham. Bentley, 1866. 2 vols. 4 illustrations.

Wives and Daughters, by Mrs. Gaskell. 2 vols. Smith, Elder, 1866. 18 illustrations.

Legends and Lyrics, by Adelaide Procter. Bell and Daldy, 1866. 2 illustrations.

The Story of a Feather, by Douglas Jerrold. Bradbury and Evans, 1867. 30 illustrations and many initial letters.

A Dark Night's Work, by Mrs. Gaskell. Smith, Elder, 1867. 4 illustrations including frontispiece and title page.

The Savage Club Papers. Tinsley, 1867. 1 illustration.

North and South, by Mrs. Gaskell. Smith, Elder, 1867. 4 illustrations including frontispiece and title page.

The History of Henry Esmond, by W. M. Thackeray. Smith, Elder, 1868. 8 full-page illustrations including frontispiece; 12 illustrations in text.

Sooner or Later, by Shirley Brooks. 2 vols. Bradbury and Evans, 1868. 17 illustrations including 2 vignettes.

Lucile, by Owen Meredith. Chapman and Hall, 1868. 24 illustrations.

Pictures from English Literature. Cassell, Petter, and Galpin, 1870. 1 illustration.

At Odds, by Baroness Tautphoeus. Bentley, 1873. 2 illustrations including vignette.

Misunderstood, by Florence Montgomery. Bentley, 1874. 8 illustrations.

Round About the Islands, by Clement Scott. Tinsley, 1874. 2 illustrations (vignette and frontispiece).

Patricia Kemball, by E. Lynn Linton. Chatto and Windus, 1875. Frontispiece.

Poor Miss Finch, The Moonstone, The New Magdalen, The Frozen Deep by Wilkie Collins. Chatto and Windus, 1875. 1 illustration in each volume.

Songs of Many Seasons, by Jemmett Browne. Simpkin, 1876. 2 illustrations.

Hurlock Chase, by G. E. Sargent. Religious Tract Society, 1876. 13 illustrations.

Pegasus Re-Saddled, by Cholmondeley Pennell. King, 1877. 10 illustrations.

Thackeray's Ballads. Smith, Elder, 1879. 10 illustrations.

Prudence: A Story of Aesthetic London, by Lucy C. Lillie. Sampson, Low, 1882. 6 illustrations.

Strange Stories, by Grant Allen. Chatto and Windus, 1884. 1 illustration.

The Black Poodle, by W. Anstey. Longmans, 1884. 1 illustration.

As in a Looking Glass, by F. C. Philips. Ward and Downey, 1889. 14 illustrations including vignette.

Peter Ibbetson, by George Du Maurier. 2 vols. Osgood, McIlvaine, 1892. 86 illustrations.

Trilby, by George Du Maurier. 3 vols. Osgood, McIlvaine, 1894. 120 illustrations.

The Martian, by George Du Maurier. *Harper*, 1898. 48 illustrations.

Index